Business Management for the Hairdresser,
Beauty and Holistic Therapist

by the same author

Beauty Therapy Fact File

Business Management for the Hairdresser, Beauty and Holistic Therapist

Susan Cressy

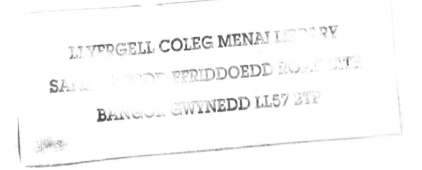
BUTTERWORTH
HEINEMANN

To Richard, Hannah, Sarah and Thomas

Butterworth-Heinemann
Linacre House, Jordan Hill, Oxford OX2 8DP
A division of Reed Educational and Professional
Publishing Ltd

ℛ A member of the Reed Elsevier plc group

OXFORD BOSTON JOHANNESBURG
MELBOURNE NEW DELHI SINGAPORE

First published 1996

British Library Cataloguing in Publication Data
Cressy, Susan
  Business management for the hairdresser, beauty
  and holistic therapist
  1 Hairdressing – Management
  2 Beauty, Personal – Management
  3 Beauty culture – Management
  I. Title
  646.7'2'068

ISBN 0 7506 2945 2

Composition by Scribe Design, Gillingham, Kent
Printed and bound in Great Britain by The Bath Press, Bath

Contents

Preface

The importance of business management for the hairdresser, beauty and holistic therapist has been recognized by all awarding bodies who now require a competent performance in management skills and a thorough knowledge of the running of a business as well as a high standard in practical skills.

I have used a practical approach in producing a book which is essential reading for all students working towards NVQ Levels 2 and 3. The content, which has been adapted from the business management section in *Beauty Therapy Fact File*, also provides a useful guide to postgraduate therapists, hairdressers and salon owners who wish to update their management knowledge and skills. It is also invaluable to therapists who are already in a supervisory position or are seeking promotion, and individuals wishing to establish their own business.

Susan Cressy

Acknowledgements

I would like to thank Karon Holmes of Top to Toe Beauty Salon, Cheshire, for supplying line illustrations, Depilex for supplying photographs for the text and, finally, Ragdale Hall Health Hydro, Melton Mowbray, and Clynol for supplying the cover photographs.

1 *Introduction to management*

It is becoming increasingly more important for the hairdresser, beauty and holistic therapist to acquire management skills. Such skills will enable each individual to improve their position within an organization or to start a business of their own.

All managers operate by achieving goals through the co-ordinated efforts of other people. The functions of management are basically the same for any kind of organization although they may be applied differently. The principal management functions are:

1 Planning.
2 Organizing.
3 Controlling.
4 Monitoring.

Planning

Planning is the management function of setting the objectives of a business, determining how best to achieve them, and making decisions concerning:

○ Policies.
○ Strategies.
○ Systems.
○ Procedures.
○ Standards.
○ Budgets.
○ Resources.

Planning may be:

Short term: Identifying day-to-day requirements which may be communicated verbally.
Medium term: Identifying requirements which may be needed over a longer period of time.
Long term: Involving higher level management

in strategic planning which may be recorded in a written format.

Good planning ensures satisfactory service and production, making the best use of the resources available. Staff should be kept to the minimum which allows the smooth running of the business while maintaining standards and quality.

Types of plan

Strategic plans: Plans that establish the nature of the organization's mission, objectives and strategies.
Standing plan: Plans which include policies, procedures, rules and regulations that are fixed for a long period of time.
Single use plans: Plans that serve a specific purpose for a short period of time.

The necessary considerations for planning are:

○ What, who, when, where.
○ To be flexible when making plans.
○ To produce plans in reasonable time to allow for consultation and familiarization before implementing them.
○ To offer clear directions in their achievement.

Plans must:

○ Provide adequate detail.
○ Be put into operation with ease.
○ Achieve the desired result.

Organizing

The management function of determining resources and activities required to achieve organizational objectives, combining them into a formal structure, assigning responsibility for achieving the objectives to capable individuals and giving them the authority needed to carry out their assignments.

Controlling

Controlling is the management function of implementing plans and ensuring the activities of the employees are achieving the set objectives.

Monitoring

Monitoring is the management function of determining methods for measuring performance, carrying out appraisal of systems, procedures and staff, comparing performance with established standards and taking the necessary corrective action.

Resources

Resources are used in a business to produce the activity and it is the responsibility of the management to use them effectively. The resources available are:

Human: The employees or personnel in a business that help to achieve its goals. It is important to provide the right type and number of employees.
Capital: Money invested in a business to set up or expand.
Equipment: Used to provide the services offered must be up-to-date, of good quality and appropriate to the requirements of the business.
Time: The manager's time and time of the employees must be used effectively. Therefore, planning and delegation are important so this valuable resource is not wasted.

The management role

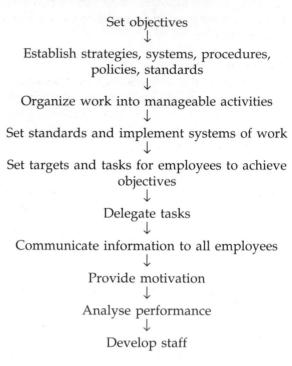

Set objectives
↓
Establish strategies, systems, procedures, policies, standards
↓
Organize work into manageable activities
↓
Set standards and implement systems of work
↓
Set targets and tasks for employees to achieve objectives
↓
Delegate tasks
↓
Communicate information to all employees
↓
Provide motivation
↓
Analyse performance
↓
Develop staff

Figure 1.1   *The role of management*

Setting objectives

Objectives are the end results towards which all organizational activities are aimed.
Before establishing objectives it is important to analyse the business:

○   What it is achieving now.
○   What your goals are.
○   How you will achieve your goals.
○   What obstacles may stand in your way.

The current position of the business may be analysed by using a SWOT analysis and it will be the start of the planning process. The analysis will provide information about the business in terms of its:

○   Strengths.
○   Weaknesses.
○   Opportunities.
○   Threats.

Strengths
Strengths are the good points which contribute to a business's success. They may include

committed and highly qualified staff, excellent facilities, well-established business with a large clientele or new technology not yet available to the competition.

Weaknesses

The problems the business may have at present are called weaknesses and they may include high staff turnover, ineffective management, limited services offered, poor facilities, lack of resources, over borrowing or high rent and rates.

Opportunities

Opportunities that may arise may include a rival salon closing down, new technology becoming available, new staff with specialist skills being employed, or an unexpected windfall.

Threats

Anything that may arise to hinder a business's plans which must be avoided at all costs can be classed as a threat.

The results of a SWOT analysis will provide useful information when making any decisions, setting objectives or business planning.

Establishing objectives for your business

The main objectives for the hairdressing, holistic and beauty manager are:

○ To provide a service efficiently and effectively.
○ To make the best use of resources.
○ To maximize profit.
○ To benefit the workforce.

The objectives should be achieved in a safe working environment to meet legal requirements.

When a business fails to provide a service which meets the requirements of its clients they will no longer patronize the establishment, and there will be no profits. The manager therefore must:

○ Establish what resources are available to achieve the objectives set and employ the appropriate number of staff with the best qualifications to ensure the highest standard of service.

○ Communicate information to employees of company policies, procedures and changes to be made at regular staff meetings or through other specified channels of communication.
○ Set targets and delegate responsibilities to individual employees, discuss methods of appraisal.
○ Establish and maintain a professional relationship with product and equipment suppliers to ensure quality of service for your clients at a reasonable cost to the business.
○ Take disciplinary action when necessary to maintain quality of service.
○ Plan and implement marketing strategies to reach the appropriate consumers for the services you offer.
○ Be prepared to change direction by keeping abreast of new innovations and treatments and develop and motivate staff to cope with change.
○ Implement efficient systems to cope with the day-to-day running of the business and ensure that quality standards are maintained.

Quality control

This is the process by which management will ensure that its services meet the expectations of clients and consumers. To maintain quality standards, all employees should be involved and the following procedures should be followed:

○ Identify any problems.
○ Discuss problems with employees.
○ Plan for improvement.
○ Implement solutions/changes.
○ Evaluate results.
○ If successful make the changes permanent.

Working as a team

Most successful businesses will have a hard working and effective team or number of teams depending upon how many employees there are. Self-managing work teams are groups that tend to operate by member consensus rather than management directions. The team can be most effective when each member understands his/her own role and fulfils that role to the best of their ability.

To be most effective there are many things that need to be considered, some of which are:

○ Meetings must be held on a regular basis for group discussion and decision making.
○ Strengths of each member should be recognized and used appropriately.
○ Work must be allocated fairly and evenly utilizing the skills available.
○ When problems occur feedback to other members of the team must be immediate, remedial action must be taken or problems must be referred upward to the line manager if nothing is resolved.
○ Flexibility is required to cope with changing circumstances.

When problems do occur a list should be made of jobs to be done in order of priority and the team must work together to determine who does what to overcome the difficulties. Staffing levels are more easily maintained when all team members are able to cover for others and work flexibly adjusting the rotas when necessary.

Useful terminology

Budget: A detailed plan or forecast, generally expressed in monetary terms, of the results expected from an officially recognized programme of operations.

Marketing: The end results, goals or targets that an organization, department or individual seeks to attain.

Objectives: The management process of identifying, anticipating and satisfying consumer requirements profitably.

Organization: Group or individuals with a common goal bound together by a set of authority/responsibility relationships needed to reach objectives.

Planning: Process of establishing objectives or goals and determining how best to attain them.

Policies: General statements that serve as guides to managerial decision-making and to supervising the activities of employees.

Procedures: Detailed plans that establish a standard or routine method or technique for handling recurring activities.

Projects: Plans for the execution of individual segments of a general programme.

Rules and regulations: Guidelines that state specifically what can and cannot be done under any given circumstances.

SWOT analysis: The process of systematically identifying and analysing an organization's strengths and weaknesses, opportunities and threats.

2 *Effective management*

The manager

The manager is responsible to the employer to achieve all the objectives laid down for the success of the business, through efficient administration and creating a good working atmosphere for all the staff employed in the business, ensuring that everyone works well as a team.

The qualities of a good manager are:

○ Commitment to the job.
○ Responsibility.
○ Enthusiasm.
○ Being decisive.
○ Using initiative.
○ Being enterprising.
○ Having patience.
○ Good judgement.
○ Integrity.

The main activities of a manager are:

1 To plan how the business is run.
2 To implement the plans.
3 To direct.
4 To coordinate.
5 To train.
6 To delegate responsibility.
7 To deal with problems.
8 To counsel.

To be successful a business needs a good leader who can communicate well with the staff, clients and business associates. The task of a manager is to get things done through people for whom they are responsible, so it is important that the manager has a good relationship with the staff to bring out the best in them.

To become an effective manager there are several important areas to be considered:

Communication

Communication may be defined as the process of creating, transmitting and interpreting ideas, opinions and facts. There are many ways in which we communicate:

○ Speaking to each other.
○ Using a telephone and fax machine.
○ Giving instructions.
○ Chairing meetings.
○ Holding interviews.
○ Sending memos.
○ Writing reports.
○ Making a presentation.

Methods of communication

Verbal: Oral communication.
Non-verbal: Use of body language, gestures and facial expressions.
Written: Letters, memos, reports, etc.

Each of these methods have advantages and disadvantages.

Verbal
Advantages
○ Instant communication.
○ Personalized.
○ May be re-inforced by non-verbal communication.
○ Quick.
○ Provides instant feedback.
○ Opportunity for clarification.

Disadvantages
○ Percentage of the information will be forgotten.
○ No point of reference later.
○ Lacks the considered nature of written communications.

Non-verbal
Advantages
○ Conveys a silent message.
○ Can be used when silence is required.

Disadvantages
o Open to misinterpretation.

Written
Advantages
o Permanent.
o Less liable to be misinterpreted.
o Information may be absorbed at the reader's own pace.
o Evidence that message has been sent.
o Ideal for important, detailed or complicated information.
o May be referred to at a later date.

Disadvantages
o Takes time to produce.
o Impersonal.
o No opportunity for questioning.
o Possibility that it may not be received.

Prepare the message/information

↓

Select the method of communication

↓

Send the message/information

↓

Check it has been accepted and understood

Figure 2.1 *The process of communication*

It is important to keep staff informed about the business, how it will develop and what part each member of staff has to play in this development.

When a member of the staff is achieving good results or working particularly well, then it is important for the manager to praise their efforts as this is an important motivating factor.

Communication is a two-way thing and the manager must always be available to listen to anything a member of staff might have to say. Regular staff meetings are an ideal way to keep the staff informed and to allow them to contribute, with comments about the way the business is run and how improvements may be made or anything they want changing, to create a happier or more comfortable work place.

The manager must then pass on these views to the owner, who may find the information useful when formulating future plans, or to other managers in the organization, as it may encourage exchange of information for mutual benefit.

Meetings

Meetings may be formal, following set procedures, with a chairperson to control the activity and other elected officers with special roles. Informal meetings have unwritten rules and procedures and more self discipline is required to ensure that results are achieved. The manager will normally take on the role of chairperson or 'leader' in a staff meeting to provide direction and ensure that time is not wasted. A successful meeting will depend upon:

o How the people present behave.
o The atmosphere in which the meeting is held.
o Whether the communication is effective.
o How large the meeting is.

All employees should be encouraged to attend meetings by:

o Holding them at the same time so that everyone is aware of when they will be held.
o Planning the content and making it relevant.
o Provide an agenda which goes out on time (Figure 2.2).
o Keep to the time allocated.
o Any other business raised must be dealt with in the time allocated or put forward to the next meeting.
o The outcome of the meeting should be implemented as soon as possible by the individuals concerned or those enlisted to take action.

Leadership

The manager is responsible for the work of all of the staff as well as his/her own. This can be very rewarding when everything is running smoothly and the business is doing well. However, if things go wrong and staff are not achieving the objectives laid down, then the manager will receive the criticism and be responsible for putting things right.

TOP TO TOE HEALTH AND BEAUTY SALON

MEETING: Monthly

FROM: Karon

TO: All staff

VENUE: Manager's office

DATE: 14.2.96 — 2p.m.

A G E N D A

SUBJECT	INCLUDED BY	RESULT/ACTION	BY WHOM
DETAILS OF VISIT TO HEALTH + BEAUTY SHOW	KH		
TRAINING DATES FOR NON. SURG. FACE LIFT	SC		
SUGGESTIONS FOR COLOUR SCHEME FOR NEW REFLEXOLOGY ROOM	KH		
APPOINTMENT OF HEALTH + SAFETY REPRESENTATIVE	KH		
ORGANISATION OF PROMOTIONAL EVENING	CP		

EXAMPLE AGENDA

Figure 2.2 *An example of an agenda*

It is important to set a good example and work to the same high standards that are set for the staff.

Delegate responsibility to those most capable but ensure that no one person is left out, by giving them a job to be responsible for, which is within their capabilities. Delegation will free the manager for other constructive work and it also helps with developing staff potential and developing further skills.

The manager is a team leader and the staff are part of that team so it is important for them to know that they can trust him/her to represent their views fairly when in any sort of dispute.

Effective leaders:

○ Have a positive self image.
○ Have a genuine ability.
○ Have realistic aspirations.
○ Have a confident approach.
○ Appreciate their own strengths and weaknesses.
○ Have vision and commitment.
○ Are expert in their field.
○ Are creative and innovative.
○ Sense change and respond to it.

Styles of leadership

Autocrat
An autocrat is a leader who makes all the decisions alone and then informs the employees what they must do. This style of management may lead to dissatisfaction and low levels of motivation. It is a style that is necessary in certain circumstances, for example the armed forces, where orders must be obeyed instantly.

Democratic
This type of leader will consult with others before making decisions, the group will be involved in setting objectives, establishing strategies and allocating jobs. Consequently the participation by employees will result in motivated staff who will work harder. The manager will need good communications skills to be successful and ensure decisions are made without lengthy consultation.

Laissez-fair
The leader is permissive and allows the employees freedom to carry out activities in any way they wish within broad limits. This creates a relaxed atmosphere but some employees do not perform well without guidelines and directions.

Discipline

Rules and regulations have to be laid down and strictly adhered to. If they are flouted by some members of staff and they are allowed to get away with it the manager's authority will be greatly weakened.

Whatever the problem, it is important to be seen to be fair and impartial so that the respect of the remaining members of staff is not lost. To prevent problems occurring, make sure that each member of staff pulls their weight and do not wait for other staff members to point this out, as it will already have caused dissatisfaction.

When having to discipline a member of staff do it in private to avoid embarrassment. Deal with the problem yourself unless it is deemed beyond your experience when you may confer with your superior.

When confronted with a problem there are certain things to be done to solve it:

○ Define the problem and recognize the priorities.
○ Decide on possible solutions.
○ Choose the solution which seems most appropriate.
○ Ensure the solution is practicable, if not look at the alternatives.
○ If necessary confer with any person involved, for example the owner, before suggesting the final solution.
○ Record the content of all interviews.

Training

It is assumed that when the position of manager has been reached you will have many skills which can be passed on to your staff which will benefit the business.

A good manager will recognize the potential of a member of staff, point them in the right direction and allow them to progress. The manager can therefore devise training programmes and implement them either in the salon or arrange for the training elsewhere.

Training will be carried out at all times in the work place as all the staff should be familiar with the day-to-day running of the business and the manager will be responsible for this, unless a particular member of staff has been delegated to deal with this area.

Induction of new employees is an important part of a manager's job, as their first impressions often have an impact on their approach to their work. Induction should not be for the first day only, it should carry on until new employees are confident about the job and feel part of the team.

An employee may have certain skills when first employed and the terms of their contract may have stated that further training would be given. The manager must ensure that these terms are met.

Working

The work carried out must be of a high standard as this will set an example to the rest of the staff. It is important to do a fair share of the practical work without doing too much so that some members of staff are sitting about idly.

Employees will learn a great deal from watching more experienced staff at work and how to treat clients to ensure their loyalty.

Counselling

Normally the manager of the business will be the first person to be approached by a member of staff with a problem. If the manager is seen to be accessible and approachable then members of staff will find it easy to come with their problems, whether they are to do with work or their personal life. The important thing to remember is to listen and make the time to listen.

Often problems can be solved by the member of staff if you, as manager, just listen and act as a sounding board. Make suggestions without actually providing a solution to the problem, as the solution you suggest may not be the correct one, then the staff member may blame you for the wrong outcome.

Anything said to you in private should remain so, as you will soon lose their confidence if you discuss their problems with others.

Organizing

Any group of people who are working together to achieve a given objective work far more effectively and efficiently if they are organized well.

The manager takes on the role of organizer so that all the resources are used most effectively. The resources available are:

o People (human resources).
o Money (financial).
o Equipment/products (material).
o Services.
o Time.

These resources may be quite substantial depending on the size of the business. The organizing role therefore will be the full-time occupation of the manager. In a smaller business the manager's time may be divided between organizing and working with the clients. In this case delegation is important so that the manager's time may be used most efficiently.

There is a limit to the number of people a manager can effectively control, therefore the appropriate span of control - the number of subordinates directly controlled by a superior - will depend on a number of factors:

o Are any subordinates qualified to make decisions without having to constantly refer upwards to the manager?
o Do they have the skills required to take the right course of action and see it through?
o Is the manager prepared to delegate authority to other employees?
o Does the business have a well-defined agreed set of objectives?

A manager may be able to control and organize a larger number of employees when the communication systems work efficiently and quickly feeds information between employees, supervisors and management. Some businesses depend a great deal on personal contact to operate effectively particularly when dealing with the public. These businesses inevitably will have small spans of control.

The manager will delegate by giving authority to an employee to perform certain tasks and responsibilities and make their own decisions

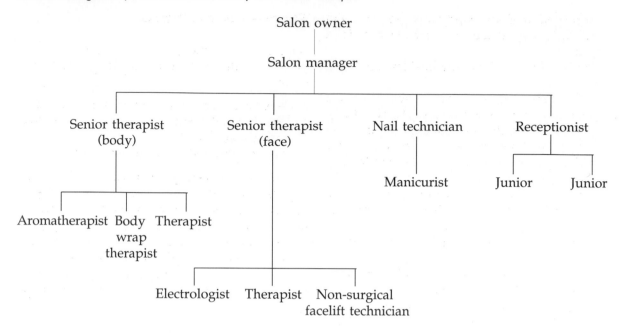

Figure 2.3 *Example of line management*

without having to refer back. Successful delegation requires:

○ Adequate authority being given to allow tasks to be carried out.
○ Specifying limits of authority.
○ Understanding by the employee of what is involved.
○ The employee to know that his/her authority and position are not duplicated elsewhere.

Advantages of delegation
○ It will highlight those employees who are suitable candidates for promotion.
○ It is useful for training purposes.
○ It develops potential.
○ It allows the most skilled person to perform a particular job.
○ It frees the manager to perform more important tasks.

Delegating tasks to employees makes good business sense as it will be more cost-effective and it provides job satisfaction for the employee, leaving the manager to be more effective. The line of authority must be clear cut so that all employees will know where they stand, that is, to whom they are responsible and who they are responsible for. Where an employee has responsibility to

one clearly defined superior the less likely it is that there will be conflicting instructions.

Line management refers to the direct working relationship between the vertical levels of an organization. This is the most common type of relationship where authority flows from the top level down to the most junior position.

Communication channels are clear, authority is agreed, instructions and information flows between the individuals concerned.

Motivating staff

Motivation is a process of encouraging an individual or group to achieve the objectives of an organization or business while also working to achieve their own objectives and ambitions. Motivation encourages employees to perform more effectively and become more productive.

A good manager will have a good understanding of the requirements of each person working within the business, as each person's needs and objectives are different.

Motivated staff are happy staff and this will ensure that they remain with the business for a long time.

The benefits of this to any business are:

o *Continuity* – as staff are familiar with the objectives of the business and all procedures, time is not wasted on training new staff and clients will not be lost when staff leave. Other members of staff can take over the role of another with little disruption.
o *Efficiency* – as the business will be run smoothly with staff familiar with company procedures and policies.
o *Teamwork* – it allows a good team to evolve who will work together and capitalize on the particular skills of each individual member of staff for the benefit of everyone.
o It provides a familiar environment for clients who feel at ease with therapists they have known for a long time.
o It inspires confidence in the clients.
o It allows a professional working relationship with suppliers to evolve which will contribute to the efficiency of the business in relation to stock control, retail sales and the provision of new products and treatments.
o It provides a good advertisement for the business when the staff turnover is low.
o High employee performance ensures a healthy turnover and profit.
o Plans can be made with the certainty that the staff who implement new policies and procedures will be available to carry them out.

Managers must provide the right environment to stimulate improved performance and develop the potential of each employee. Increased performance relies on a combination of ability and motivation, ability alone is not enough to improve productivity, strong motivation with improved ability achieves results.

Even when there is a climate of positive motivation provided by the management there must be motivation from within each individual to improve performance. When the abilities of each employee are used efficiently this should result in increased productivity and job satisfaction.

Theories of motivation

Content theories – needs
These are theories of motivation which deal with:

o What causes behaviour to occur and to cease.
o The internal needs and perceptions of the individual.
o The external factors such as incentives.

Maslow's hierarchy of needs is the most popular of content theories. The psychologist Abraham Maslow's concept was that human needs may be arranged in a hierarchy of importance progressing from basic needs at the bottom to higher needs at the top and that a satisfied need was no longer a prime motivator of behaviour. These needs are shown in Figure 2.4.

Self-actualization needs
|
Esteem needs
|
Social needs
|
Safety needs
|
Physiological needs

Figure 2.4 *Hierarchy of needs*

The hierarchy begins with:
Physiological needs: For example food, drink and sleep. The manager provides these needs through wages, holidays, provision of adequate staff facilities, a healthy environment, clean drinking water, lunch breaks and rests.
Safety needs: For example, protection against danger, threat or deprivation and the provision of a stable environment. The manager provides these through ensuring a safe and secure working environment, health insurance, staff development, promotion prospects, saving plans and pension schemes.
Social needs: For example, belonging, association with and acceptance by colleagues, giving and receiving love. The manager provides these by creating formal and informal teams that work well together, company sponsored activities and

providing status for employees through delegation.

Esteem needs: For example, status, self-esteem, recognition and appreciation. The manager provides these through promotion, praise, commendation and reward.

Self-actualization needs: For example, achieving one's potential, achieving ambitions and self-development. The manager may help by setting targets and goals, providing challenges, setting assignments and developing skills.

Herzberg's motivation–hygiene theory

Herzberg's theory was based on information provided by employees about job satisfaction. His initial research was based on answers provided by several hundred engineers and accountants about their jobs. Further studies were then carried out with other working groups including clerical and manual workers, the results from each group were similar.

The factors which provided the employees with job satisfaction were motivators (motivating factors) and those that caused dissatisfaction were demotivators (hygiene factors).

Motivators – motivating factors
○ Achievements.
○ Recognition received.
○ The creative and challenging nature of the work.
○ The responsibility given.
○ Opportunities for personal growth.
○ Promotion.

Demotivators – hygiene factors
○ Company policy and administration which stifles enthusiasm.
○ Poor quality of supervision – technical aspects.
○ Salary.
○ Interpersonal relations.
○ Working conditions.
○ Working environment and lack of benefits.

The conclusions of his research were that motivating factors which gave job satisfaction had a positive effect on performance and morale and factors which caused job dissatisfaction had a negative effect.

Based on these theories and in simple terms the employer/manager must try to ensure that the employee has:

○ A fair and acceptable wage system.
○ Job security.
○ Generous holidays.
○ Varied work experience.
○ Flexibility of working hours.
○ Training to develop further skills.
○ To be given responsibility with a certain amount of independence.
○ The opportunity for personal growth and achievement.
○ Compatibility with colleagues.
○ An opportunity to be part of a successful team.
○ Safe and secure working conditions.
○ Good staff facilities.
○ Recognition and praise for good work.
○ Prospects of promotion.

Interviewing

An interview is communicating with someone to achieve a specific objective, which could be selecting staff, counselling, disciplining, assessment, grievance, etc.

There are certain considerations common to all interviews and these are:

The preparation

Have available all the necessary information required and any relevant documentation. Confer beforehand with other parties with an interest in the outcome of the interview, for example the salon owner may want to put some specific points to you with regard to the interview, or another member of staff who may be involved.

The objective

Know exactly what you hope to achieve by the end of the interview, this will allow you to complete the business in hand without further time being wasted.

Conducting the interview

Move the interview towards your objective and ensure that you elicit a constructive response from the interviewee while retaining control and deciding on the action to be taken, informing the interviewee of any follow-up procedures.

Appraisal

This is an evaluation of an individual member of staff in terms of their job performance or skills. It must be fair and accurate and it may be necessary for various reasons:

○ To identify standards of job performance.
○ To identify strengths and weaknesses.
○ To identify training and development needs.
○ To identify possibilities for promotion.
○ To review salary and responsibilities.
○ To provide staff motivation.
○ To formulate business plans.

Informal assessment occurs naturally on a day-to-day basis in the workplace. The formal assessment is planned and uses a standard set of criteria to evaluate performance. A systematic approach should be adopted and the following steps should be taken:

1 Design an appropriate appraisal form.
2 Conduct an appraisal interview or observe performance in practical skills.
3 Complete an appraisal form.
4 Review the appraisal with the employee.
5 Agree on a plan of action which could be further training, promotion, an increase in salary or job improvement.

The appraisal form

When designing an appraisal form, the focus of the appraisal must be clear, that is, the job or the person. When the main focus is the job, the criteria will concentrate on such things as reaching sales targets and achieving set objectives. Where the main focus is on the person, the criteria will concentrate on personal qualities, attitude and behaviour as well as practical skills. To save time the form must be as simple to use as possible. To be effective it must have relevant performance criteria and an efficient measurement system.

Figure 2.5 is an example of a general appraisal form. When practical skills are to be assessed more specific criteria must be used. For training purposes the detailed procedure must be written down and assessed. The outcome of any appraisal must be discussed with the employee as soon as possible. In fact, if this process can be tackled as a joint problem-solving exercise between management and employees it will be far more productive working together on a more equal basis.

Figure 2.6 is an example of a practical assessment form.

Staff development

Most employees are keen to progress in their chosen line of work and their manager may assist them with their own personal objectives by providing opportunities to develop their skills and achieve their aims.

Appraisal will indicate the areas of strength and weakness of each individual employee. Using this information an action plan for training and development may be formulated. To ensure that staff development is successful there are several considerations:

○ Further training and development must be agreed mutually between the manager and employee.
○ The actions to be taken must be clear and concise so that both parties understand what is required.
○ Plans must be realistic, the employee must be capable of achieving the desired results and the manager must not have unrealistic expectations.
○ A reasonable amount of time must be given to achieve the objectives before reviewing the outcome.
○ Ensure there are sufficient resources available.

TOP TO TOE HEALTH AND BEAUTY SALON
STAFF APPRAISAL

Name of employee: Position:

Period of assessment: From: To:

Assessment criteria	1 Unsatisfactory	2 Average	3 Above average	4 Outstanding	Score
1 Organization skills					
2 Quality of work					
3 Reaching sales targets					
4 Initiative					
5 Teamwork					
6 Communication skills					
7 Adaptability					
				Total	

Score
 1–12   Unsatisfactory
13–18   Average
19–25   Above average
26–28   Outstanding

Comments:

Action:

Assessor:_____

Employee:_____

Date:_____

Figure 2.5 *An appraisal form*

TOP TO TOE HEALTH AND BEAUTY SALON
PRACTICAL ASSESSMENT

Name of employee: Position:

Date of assessment:

Treatment:

Assessment criteria	Satisfactory	Above average	Excellent	Comments
Preparation of work area				
Health and safety procedures				
Client care and consideration				
Practical procedure				
Recording treatment				
Homecare advice				
Recommendations				

Action taken: Assessor signature:

_____

Employee signature:

_____

Figure 2.6 *An assessment form*

○ Always use the most effective methods of development.
○ Ensure that the recommended action will contribute to:
  –employees own personal objectives.
  –business objectives.
  –team objectives.

Disciplinary procedures

One of the more difficult areas of staff management is dealing with disciplinary issues. The aim of discipline is to correct behaviour and the last resort is to penalize a member of staff. Therefore the best way of dealing with problems of discipline is to prevent them occurring in the first place.

To do this the manager must:

○ Explain to each new member of staff exactly what is expected of them.
○ Set standards in job performance which have to be met.
○ Lay down a fair set of rules and regulations which all members of staff will follow.
○ Explain the reason for the rules.

Rules can cover many areas and the more important ones for the smooth running of a salon are:

Punctuality

Each member of staff must arrive for work at the designated time and ready for the first appointment. There is little point arriving for work on time and then spending half an hour changing into work clothes and applying makeup while the first client is sitting waiting as this will upset the appointment system for the rest of the day.

In the case of genuine illness, the employee must inform the manager at the earliest possible time to allow him/her to contact clients to change their appointments or for replacement members of staff to be called in.

Behaviour

A professional approach is required in dealing with clients and other members of staff.

Treatment of clients is important as a friendly but respectful manner will encourage loyalty and ensure the client returns. Respect should be shown for senior members of staff and all employees should work together as a team.

Safety

Rules regarding health and safety at work include hygiene and maintenance of the salon, handling hazardous substances and being responsible for the safety of clients and other members of staff. It is the responsibility of the manager to make everyone aware of their own responsibilities in these areas.

Company property

The appearance of the salon is important as this often forms a lasting impression in the mind of a client. Staff should be responsible for their own particular work area as well as having joint responsibility for communal areas, in particular the reception area and for staff comfort, the staff room.

Company property must not be abused and telephones should not be used for personal calls as this ties up the telephone when prospective clients may be ringing. It also costs the business money.

Stock

Certain people should be responsible for care and maintenance of stock and to prevent pilferage. Special concessions may be made to staff, for example buying at cost price or at a generous discount to prevent pilferage.

Disciplinary action

The procedure to follow for breaches of discipline are dealt with in detail in Chapter 3. Disciplinary action should only be taken if there is clear evidence of a serious breach of the rules and any action must be fair and consistent with the misdemeanour.

When giving an employee a verbal warning it is advisable to do so in front of a third person and then write an account for the records. The member of staff concerned has the right to appeal against disciplinary action.

The manager must ensure that all members of staff have access to their job descriptions, a list of all rules and regulations and the disciplinary procedures set down.

To prevent industrial tribunals or other legal actions, follow strict guidelines for disciplinary procedures. Guidelines can be obtained from your local branch of ACAS.

To summarize, the guidelines propose that disciplinary procedures should be in written form; they may be included in the written terms and conditions of employment; in a staff handbook, displayed in the work place or available to the employee in an easily accessible file.

○ They must specify to whom they apply.
○ They must be capable of dealing speedily with disciplinary matters to avoid disruption, maintain staff morale and allow the management time to concentrate on more important matters.
○ They must indicate the form of disciplinary action which may be taken.
○ They must specify who will deal with disciplinary action.
○ They must state how an individual will be informed of their misconduct.
○ They must allow for proper investigation.
○ They must state how an individual will be informed of disciplinary action.
○ They must provide for a right of appeal.

Organizing your time efficiently

There are so many jobs for a manager that it can be easy to neglect certain aspects of the work. It is important, therefore, to sit down and analyse the time being spent on each area of responsibility.

Start by making a list of each job that must be done, for example:

○ Paperwork.
○ Training.

○ Practical application of treatments.
○ Stock control.
○ Business meetings.
○ Planning.
○ Interviewing.

Then rearrange the list in order of importance to you and the approximate time you devote each week to that task.

Ask yourself the following questions

1 Are you spending enough time on the more important matters?
2 Can the time spent on less important activities be reduced?
3 Are there any activities which you can delegate?
4 Can you eliminate any activities?

Make a chart of jobs that have to be done:

○ Daily.
○ Weekly.
○ At longer intervals.

The simpler the system of recording when jobs must be done, the easier it will be and nothing should be overlooked. The options are to:

1 *Keep a large wall calendar* and record regular activities, special jobs, appointments, etc.
2 *Keep a desk diary* which has a separate page for each day and record the same information as the wall calendar but with additional room for more detail.

Work out a daily routine for:

○ *The start of the day*
  –Check the appointment book.
  –Deal with any problems regarding staff, lateness, absenteeism.
  –Check that the salon and all treatment areas are prepared.
  –Switch on all necessary equipment, for example saunas.
  –Check equipment.
  –Check the stock details.
  –Carry on with any other work.
○ *The end of the day*
  –Consider problems which have arisen during the day.
  –Consider the action required to deal with the problems.

–Look at jobs which have to be done the next day.
–Work out an approximate timetable.
–Anticipate problems which may arise and make arrangements to cope with them.

Insurance cover

One of the priorities for any business is to provide insurance cover against all risks. Some insurance is required by law and there is general insurance, some of which is relevant only to your own business. Being under-insured, or failing to insure, could cause serious financial problems by using cash resources to meet uninsured losses.

When taking out insurance it is important to ensure that the cover is adequate otherwise it is a waste of money. Insurance may be obtained from:

o   The insurance company directly.
o   An insurance broker.
o   A solicitor or accountant.
o   The bank.

Insurance companies

Companies who sell insurance, sell directly to the public or through insurance brokers or agents. Some companies specialize in certain types of insurance and others will provide a comprehensive range of insurance.

Insurance broker

A broker is an impartial adviser who deals with all the insurance companies, providing every type of policy. Brokers are required by their code of conduct to put your interests as a client above all others so they will probably be the best source of insurance. Professional advice is usually given free and without obligation.

Solicitor or accountant

There are solicitors and accountants who may work full time with insurance and may have the title agent, consultant or financial adviser.

It may be convenient to consult a professional that you already work with. However, the solicitor or the accountant may deal with a limited number of insurance companies and there is a chance that you may not receive the best quote, or know that you are dealing with a company that has a good record in paying claims.

Bank

The bank manager or insurance adviser will explain the type of insurance your business will require and the probable cost. Most banks will provide insurance. However, they may only deal with a limited number of insurance companies unless they specifically act as an insurance broker themselves, then they will have to follow the code of conduct, putting your interests before all other considerations.

Types of insurance

There is a large range of insurance policies available for small businesses and package policies can be arranged which will provide all the insurance required for your business. The following are the most frequently used types of insurance protection:

Fire

Buildings and their contents can be insured against fire damage.

Special perils

If it is thought necessary 'special perils' may be added. These can include explosion, impact by aircraft, riot and malicious damage, impact by vehicles, storm, flood, bursting or overflowing of water tanks and pipes. It would be advisable to insure against storm and flood damage if the premises are located in a coastal area.

All risks

This is a much wider cover. In addition to the above it also includes any accidental damage or loss not specifically excluded by the insurance company. The exclusions which will be stated in the policy are things such as:

○ Wear and tear.
○ Electrical breakdown.
○ Gradual deterioration.

Theft

Providing there has been forcible entry to, or exit from the premises, contents are usually insured against loss from theft. Policies should include damage to the building as a result of the theft. Theft by employees or shoplifters is not normally included in this policy.

Fidelity

This type of insurance compensates the employer for loss of money or goods as a result of an act of dishonesty by an employee.

Money

Cover will apply to the theft of cash, cheques and certain other negotiable documents. There are different limits which apply to:

○ Money on the premises.
○ In and out of business hours.
○ In safes.
○ At the homes of directors or employees.
○ In transit.

Consequential loss

Business may be interrupted or come to a complete standstill as a result of any of the above. This will lead to a loss of income and possibly other expenses incurred in trying to maintain the business. This policy will compensate for the loss of income so that ongoing business expenses can be met.

Liability

There are three different types of liability:

Employers' liability

This insurance is required by law so that you are insured against injury to employees or illness as a result of the work undertaken.

You are also required by law to exhibit a certificate of employers' liability insurance at your place of work. The premium you will pay for this type of insurance will be related to the size of the payroll and the risks attached to the jobs.

Public liability

This provides insurance cover against injury or illness caused by your business to any member of the public. It also covers legal fees and costs that may be incurred as a result of a claim against you.

Product liability

If the business manufactures or sells products, as a beauty salon most probably will, then you could be held legally liable for any injury which may occur arising from product defects. Product liability insurance provides the necessary cover.

Credit

Credit insurance will protect your business against clients failing to pay but this insurance is not easily available unless you have a well established business.

Legal expenses

In the event of a contractual or employment dispute these policies will provide cover for the legal expenses.

Life insurance

If the death of a member of your staff would actually cost the business money, as that person's expertise and knowledge was crucial to the running of the business, it would be worthwhile arranging 'key personnel' insurance to cover the cost of replacing the employee.

Permanent health insurance

This insurance provides for a continuation of income in the event of ill health or accident preventing you or an employee from working for a period of time or permanently.

Personal accident and sickness

These policies are renewable annually and provide cover for incapacity caused by accident or ill health.

Buying insurance

The insurance company will probably carry out a survey of the premises before providing cover and will draw attention to any potential hazards and advise on ways to reduce the risk.

The proposal form

This must be filled in to provide the insurance company with all the information they require. This will include:

- The name and address of the proposer.
- The type of business.
- Details of previous losses.
- Insurance history.
- Details of the risk to be insured.

Duty of disclosure

Any person applying for insurance is obliged to disclose to the insurer all the relevant facts which might affect the risk insured or the terms of acceptance, for example the premium. Failure to comply could entitle the insurer to treat the policy as invalid.

The policy

The insurance policy is a document which sets out all the details of the contract.

Premium

The premium is the payment for insurance which may be paid annually or by instalments during the period for which insurance cover is provided.

3 Human resource management

Human resource management is an important management function as the staff employed in the beauty, holistic and hairdressing industry are providing a personal service so they must have the right qualifications, appearance, manner and approach to their work. The client–therapist relationship once established can be an enduring one. Therefore, choosing the best therapists and investing time and effort into training and development can prove profitable to any business. There are many factors to consider:

o Recruitment and selection.
o Induction and training.
o Promotion.
o Appraisal.
o Discipline.
o Working conditions.
o Career development.

When operating a beauty business, finding the right staff is extremely important as constant changes will adversely affect the business.

Clients who attend regularly for treatment usually return to the same therapist or hairdresser each time, once a professional client–therapist relationship has developed.

A good therapist soon gains the confidence of the client and will therefore generate a great deal of business for the salon owner.

When looking for staff it is important to make sure that the right person for the job is chosen first time because hiring the wrong staff and then having to re-advertise will be disruptive to the business.

Recruitment

The objective of recruitment is to attract the 'best' people for the job and then to choose the most suitable. It is important therefore to be clear about:

o What the job entails.
o What qualities are required of the person to do the job.
o What is needed to retain and motivate staff.

It is important to draw up a job description which provides details of the job, the specific tasks and duties. It should include:

o Job title, such as manager, aromatherapist, nail technician or senior stylist.
o A brief description of the main purpose of the job.
o Specific tasks or responsibilities.
o Responsible to, for example, supervisor, manager, owner.
o Responsible for, for example, other employees.

The purpose of the job description is:

o It provides information to prospective employees.
o It helps to identify the requirements for each job.
o It forms the basis of job evaluation for payment of wages.
o Disputes about work an employee is asked to do may be settled by looking at the job description.

Example of a job description

The salon is relatively new and there are four therapists, all with little industrial experience, currently working with the owner. The owner now requires a manager to help in the plans to increase business and motivate existing staff. The job description for a salon manager would include the following details:

Title: Salon manager.

Aim: Increase the clientele and help to expand the business. To be responsible for four members of staff.

Accountability: Liaise with the salon owner.

Staff responsibility: Four fully-trained but inexperienced beauty therapists.

Duties: Organizing staff rotas.

Training staff in new techniques.

Stock controller.

Special tasks: Assisting the owner in marketing the salon and its products.

Once this has been set down you will have a clear picture of the position to be filled. It is now important to form a picture of the person you want by drawing up a job specification, which is a detailed statement of the physical and mental activities in a job.

The details required would be:

- Education.
- Specific training.
- Previous experience.
- Specialized skills.
- Personal attributes.
- Communication skills.
- Fitness and health.

Once the job description has been established a **job specification** or person specification may be drawn up. This shows a profile of the type of person required to do the job. It will establish the criteria for selecting the new employee and should include:

Attainment: Qualifications such as NVQ, other additional certificates or records of competence.

Experience: Years in industry and range of experience.

Practical skills: Including specialist areas.

Additional skills: Book-keeping, marketing etc.

Personal attributes: Mature, flexible, helpful, professional, good appearance.

Fitness/health.

Communication skills.

Personal interests.

Under normal circumstances the employee will become a full-time, permanent salaried member of staff. The beauty business, however, depending upon the treatments offered does have very busy periods when more staff are required and quiet periods when employees have little to do. It may be worthwhile therefore to look at the alternatives.

Part-time staff

When a business is new, the financial commitment of permanent, full-time members of staff may be too big a burden or the work available may not add up to a full working week. Sometimes the employees do not wish to work full-time due to other commitments and to accommodate them it may be the best course of action to offer part-time work rather than lose a competent member of the workforce.

Commission only

Working on a commission only basis will be an incentive for the therapist to increase the number of treatments per week and the amount of sales on complementary products, thus increasing the takings along with the wages. Salaried staff with a regular wage each week may only carry out the minimum amount of work required.

The two can in fact be combined quite efficiently by the employer guaranteeing a basic wage and when the employee reaches a set target figure a commission is earnt on any sales above that figure.

Freelance

There may be a time such as the pre-summer period or pre-Christmas period which are heavily booked and a therapist may be very happy to work for that period for a set fee. National insurance contributions, holiday or sick pay are the responsibility of the freelance not the therapist. The terms must be agreed at the outset that the work is temporary and for a certain period of time.

Figure 3.1 *Job advertisement*

PORTERS BEAUTY SALON
require a
SALON MANAGER

The successful candidate must hold nationally recognizable qualifications and have a minimum of 3 years experience in the industry.

Dedication and ambition is required to expand this new, modern health and beauty centre.

The ability to organize staff and take responsibility for stock control as well as patience and a sense of humour are essential.

In return we offer excellent working conditions and salary is negotiable.

Apply in writing with full curriculum vitae to:
Mrs Stewart, Porters Beauty Salon, Ashley Road, Hale, Cheshire.

Attracting staff

There are several different avenues open to you when looking for staff:

1 Advertising.
2 Recruitment agency.
3 Local college.
4 Asking colleagues, business contacts or clients.

Advertising

The main purpose of advertising is to attract the largest number of candidates with the right qualifications thereby ensuring a reasonable chance of finding the most appropriate person for the job.

This can be done locally or nationally and the response is usually fairly quick. The advertisement needs to attract the ideal candidate for your business therefore:

○ It should be appropriately placed to reach the target audience.
○ It should stimulate their interest and hold their attention.
○ It should be clear to the job applicants if they are suitable candidates for the job and that it is worth applying for.

The advertisement (see Figure 3.1) should contain:

○ The job title.
○ The salary.
○ The location.
○ The work involved.
○ The requirements.
○ Closing date for application.
○ Application contact.

Recruitment agency

This is a costly method of staff recruitment and there are few specializing in jobs within the beauty industry. The main advantage is that the agency will sift through all prospective candidates, leaving you time to run your business. The agency may also have people with special skills on their books.

Local colleges

Recruiting direct from colleges in your area would save advertising costs and hopefully the college tutors could recommend a student with the qualities and expertise that you require.

Their industrial experience would however be minimal. Therefore, it could be some time before the student would be working to full potential and contributing effectively to the business profits. It would be advisable to accept students on industrial release from college and see them working first hand before employing them full-time.

Colleagues/business contacts

This has the advantage of personal recommendations but it would be advisable to ask for a CV and carry out an interview in the normal way.

The disadvantage is that there is a possibility of missing out on a more suitable candidate by not advertising the job.

Selecting staff

When the prospective candidates reply to the advertisement it is now time to collect all the information together about each application in such a way that the unsuitable candidates will be easily eliminated.

The most efficient way to do this is to ask each candidate to fill in an application form and from this you can choose a certain number of candidates who match up with your requirements and arrange an interview with them.

The application form

The application form should make selection much easier as each applicant will provide details in the same way (Figure 3.2). The information required would include:

○ Personal details.
○ Educational qualifications.
○ Past experience.
○ Personal interests.
○ Reasons for applying for the job.
○ References.

The interview

An interview provides the opportunity to give all the necessary information about the job to the applicants and ask any questions which will help you decide which of them will be successful. There are certain considerations to be made when conducting an interview:

○ Decide in advance where the interview will be held. This is particularly important if you wish the applicant to demonstrate practical skills. The salon or treatment area will then be the ideal location. To promote a relaxed atmosphere it would be advisable to make sure the salon is not too busy at the time of the interview so that the applicant will not be overlooked or overheard.

○ Always begin by putting the applicant at ease to bring out the best in them.

○ Ensure the questions you ask will elicit the required information. Asking open questions which require more than a yes or no answer will provide you with a good idea of their communication skills and competence.

○ Specific questions should also be asked to test the applicant's knowledge of the subject.

○ When interviewing several people in a short space of time it would be useful to take notes as a source of reference when assessing all the applicants afterwards.

○ Provide interviewees with some information about the job and show them where they may be working.

○ Answer any questions interviewees might ask and provide the opportunity for them to bring out any points which may prove their suitability for the job and may not already have been covered.

○ Inform interviewees when and how they will be contacted to give them the result of the interview.

As a courtesy to those people who have responded to the job advertisement who have had an interview but have been unsuccessful an acknowledgement in the form of a letter is appropriate. A short letter to the point is all that is required, for example:

Dear Miss Jones,

Re: Vacancy for salon manager

Further to your interview on Friday, 20 September 1996, with regard to the above vacancy, I regret to inform you that on this occasion your application has not been successful.

I would like to take this opportunity to thank you for your interest shown in our salon and wish you every success in your future career.

Yours sincerely,

After the interview

Once you have decided which applicant matches up to the criteria you originally set out, by assessing all their strengths and weaknesses, their references must be checked, before finally making an offer of a job.

It can be more fruitful speaking to a referee by phone rather than contacting them by letter and trying to interpret what has been written.

The job offer should be put in writing and it should be on the condition that the references are satisfactory. This is important because once the offer has been accepted there is a contract and if references are then deemed unsatisfactory it is very difficult to remove the employee from the job.

The employer should secure the permission of the prospective employee before applying for references.

When the new employee joins your workforce set out your plans for induction and training and this will increase motivation and provide a positive start to the new job.

Induction

An induction programme will help a new employee settle in to a new job and will provide them with information about how the business works. The management should provide information about some or all of the following:

o The business – history, activity development and plans for the future.
o Policies, rules and regulations.
o Terms of employment to include disciplinary rules.

o Employee benefits and services.
o The roles of supervisors.
o Familiarization with the establishment, procedures and systems.

Induction should take place as soon as new employees start work, allowing time for them to adjust to the new social and work environment.

An experienced member of staff may be enlisted to help guide the new employee through the induction process and pass on valuable experience and knowledge, introducing the new member of staff to fellow employees and generally making them feel comfortable in their new job.

Factors which motivate staff

o A fair and equitable pay system.
o When there are opportunities for promotion.
o Varied work experience and training to develop further skills.
o To be given responsibility with a certain amount of independence.
o Praise for good work.
o Generous holidays.
o Job security.
o Flexibility in working hours.
o Being part of a successful team.

Training

Training may be for induction purposes, the training of new staff in the organization or the general and specialist training of existing employees. If a business is to grow and develop then the people within it must also grow and develop.

Generally speaking, the better developed employees cause fewer problems and have greater job satisfaction.

Reasons for training

o Induction of new employees.

APPLICATION FOR EMPLOYMENT

Thank you for applying to Top to Toe Health and Beauty Salon.
Please complete the application form in your own handwriting.

POST APPLIED FOR:

Title:_____   Surname:_____

First Name(s):_____

Address:	
	Date of Birth:_____
	Nationality:_____
	How did you hear about the vacancy?
Telephone No.:	

EDUCATION AND TRAINING:- SECONDARY, FURTHER AND PART-TIME

SCHOOL/COLLEGE ADDRESS	FROM-TO	QUALIFICATIONS	GRADE	DATE

EMPLOYMENT - PLEASE GIVE DETAILS OF THE LAST TWO EMPLOYERS

NAME & ADDRESS	FROM-TO	BRIEF JOB DESCRIPTION
1.		
2.		

Figure 3.2 *An example of an application form*

RELEVANT ADDITIONAL INFORMATION:	DO YOU HAVE A HEALTH PROBLEM/ DISABILITY?
	_____ (Yes/No)
	IF YES, PLEASE DESCRIBE:
	ARE YOU REGISTERED DISABLED?
	_____ (Yes/No)

HOBBIES AND INTERESTS:

REFERENCES - Please give the name of two referees we can contact to support the information in this application.

Name:_____   Name:_____

Address_____   Address:_____

_____   _____

_____   _____

_____   _____

Occupation:_____   Occupation:_____

I declare that the statements in this form are correct to the best of my knowledge. I understand that my engagement will be conditional upon satisfactory references and medical clearance.

Signature:_____   Date:_____

EXAMPLE APPLICATION FOR EMPLOYMENT

Figure 3.2 *Continued*

o Training in health and safety procedures to comply with current legislation.
o To introduce a new treatment or service.
o To improve product knowledge.
o To update existing skills.
o To develop knowledge or skills of employees.

Methods of training

Coaching/supervision: Explaining and supervising methods of work, procedures and systems. Normally a manager or supervisor would take on a role of developing and improving a subordinates abilities.

Planned progression: Moving the employee through a well-ordered series of jobs into increasing higher levels of activity.

Job rotation: Moving the employee through a series of diverse jobs to experience all aspects of a business and improve knowledge and experience.

Demonstrations: Learning from an expert's demonstration and performing under the guidance of an experienced person or mentor. The expert could be from a company or training institution or from among your own staff.

Training centres: An employee may attend college on a part-time basis combining more structured learning with the real work situation. Open learning enables the employee to complete a training programme devised by a college or training centre using a correspondence course or flexible learning programme to combine work and study.

Benefits of training

o Achievement of high standards in performance.
o Staff motivation.
o Job satisfaction.
o Higher quality production.
o Reduction in staff turnover.
o More flexible work force with transferable skills.
o More efficient use of human resources.
o Improved status or salary.

Training procedure

Identify training needs
↓
Establish training objectives
↓
Plan the content
↓
Arrange a time for training
↓
Provide the training
↓
Monitor and review

Figure 3.3 *The training process*

Staff rotas

A staff rota is a plan of the working hours of each member of staff. It is required to ensure that there are sufficient numbers of staff available at any given time to accommodate all the clients booked.

The rota must include:

o When staff are in the salon for work.
o When staff are on holiday.
o The times staff are out of the salon for training.
o When staff are working overtime or involved in other activities, for example marketing or promotions.
o Time off in lieu of overtime.

Considerations when planning a staff rota are:

o Which days of the week are the busiest.
o What time of the day is the busiest.
o Seasonal fluctuations – before Christmas and before summer are very busy periods of the year
o Staff requirements and special requests
o What jobs and activities need to be covered
o Which members of staff are most appropriate for the jobs

Contingency plans must be made for the unexpected:

o Staff absence due to illness.
o Staff leaving.

o An unexpected increase in business.
o An unexpected decrease in client numbers.

These problems may be overcome if:

o A number of flexible part-time members of staff who are prepared to work more hours are employed.
o If the full-time members of staff are prepared to work more hours or overtime when required.
o If a floating member of staff is employed to step into any role if it is affordable to do so.

Discrimination

To help eliminate discrimination at work there are several acts which attempt to remove any inequality in the work place.

The Equal Pay Act 1970

The main aim of this act is to eliminate discrimination on grounds of sex and to give all employees equal treatment. This should guarantee a woman:

o Equal pay for doing the same or broadly similar work as a man.
o Equality in all benefits laid down in the contract of employment.

The Sex Discrimination Act 1975

This act requires the employer not to discriminate between men and women in employment recruitment, training and all areas of employment other than pay:

o In the job advertisement.
o In the interview.
o In opportunities for promotion.

There are qualifications an employer may ask for that may indicate that a certain sex is being discriminated against but if it can be shown that these qualifications are genuinely necessary for the job there would be no case.

It is illegal to victimize any person who may take you to an industrial tribunal over sex discrimination, who has helped another person to do so or that you suspect might do so.

The Race Relations Act 1976

This act makes it unlawful to discriminate against anyone simply on the grounds of race in recruitment, training, employment and promotion.

The Commission for Racial Equality has produced a code of conduct to help eliminate racial discrimination.

Employment procedures

Once an employee starts work a contract of employment exists as the employee has accepted the employer's terms and conditions of employment. A written contract of employment must be given to the employee by the employer within thirteen weeks of starting the job. This is basically a written statement laying down the terms and conditions agreed by both parties. The items for inclusion on the statement would be:

Employer's name.
Employee's name.
The date employment commences.
The rate of pay and how it is calculated.
When payment will be made.
Working hours.
Holiday entitlement including public holidays and holiday pay.
Arrangements for absences due to sickness or injury and provisions for sick pay.
Details of pensions and pension schemes.
The period for notice of termination the employer and employee must give.
Provision for maternity leave.
The job title.
Disciplinary rules and grievance procedures.

Change in terms

The employer is obliged to inform the employee, in a further written statement, of any change in terms of employment within a month of its introduction. The employer may also meet this obligation by updating reference material which is readily accessible to the employee, as long as the reference documents are updated within one month of the change.

In the event of no written statement being given, the employee may refer the matter to an industrial tribunal. The terms which it may lay down will be as binding as those of the employer.

Example of a written statement

Terms and conditions of employment

I *Sally Hart* of *Face Facts* beauty salon, Westhampton.

am employing

Rachel Walker of 25 Clarendon Place, Norcliffe.

On:

20 June 1992

In the position of *salon manager.*

The basic weekly wage is £120. In addition 10% commission will be paid on all sales above £500.

The working hours will be:

Tuesday–Thursday 9 a.m.–5 p.m.
Friday 9 a.m.–7 p.m.
Saturday 9 a.m.–3 p.m.

Holiday entitlement will be 4 weeks per annum and all public holidays.

Payment will be made in full for any time lost through sickness or injury other than the first three days. All claims must be accompanied by a sick note.

There is no company pension scheme.

The amount of notice of termination of employment to be given by:

The employer is – two weeks.
The employee is – two weeks.

The disciplinary rules of the salon can be found in Document no. 001.

You may appeal to the *staff manager, Jenny Roberts,* to discuss any disciplinary decision.

The procedure for making your appeal is laid down in Document no. 002.

Grievances concerning employment should be made to *Sally Hart* in person.

Your solicitor could draw up a standard contract of employment and may be able to advise you on additional items to be included which are of relevance to your business, for example a radius clause.

Radius clause

This clause is to prevent a member of staff who leaves to set up in opposition, or to work for an already established salon, from taking any of your clientele.

The clause should state that the employee may not work within a specific distance for a specified length of time. The distance and time stated must not be deemed unreasonable.

Written statements need not be given to:

o   Someone who is working freelance.
o   Employees who work less than sixteen hours a week unless they have been employed for five years continuously for at least eight hours a week.

It is advisable to keep a duplicate of the written statement together with the employee's application form, a copy of your letter of offer and any notes you may have made at the interview.

The terms set out in the statement cannot be changed without the consent of both parties. In the case of promotion or a change of role, the job is not the same and therefore the employee may need a new written statement.

It is also necessary when taking on a new employee to inform your local tax office.

Payment of wages

Most employees have the right to an itemized pay statement. The details to be included are laid down by law and these briefly are:

five
pay

Di

The
an
reas
pre
disi

No

The

o

o

It
dur
ind
fair

Dis

o
o

o

o

o

o

o

1   *The gross pay*. The total amount earned by an employee before any deductions have been taken. It will include the basic pay, plus additional payments, for example commission, which is a percentage of the sales the employee has made, and overtime.

2   Any *fixed deductions* and the reason they are made itemized separately on the pay slip with a reason for each deduction.

3   The amount of *variable deductions* and the reason they are made.

4   *The net pay*. The total amount received by an employee after any deductions have been taken.

When wages are paid in cash the employee should be asked to sign your copy, as a receipt of payment.

Deductions

The deductions from the employee's wages are either laid down by law or are with the agreement of the employee.

Tax and national insurance must be deducted.

In some cases money may be deducted to enforce a court order, for example non-payment of council tax. This is called an *attachment of earnings*.

Voluntary deductions

These could be any of the following:

o   Private pension schemes, to supplement their state pension.
o   Savings.
o   Private medical scheme.

PAYE

Once you have registered with the tax office that you have become an employer, they will send you tax and national insurance contribution tables which will show you how much tax and national insurance must be deducted from the employee's wages.

A deductions working sheet is then made up for each employee. This is filled in for each pay day.

Tax and national insurance contributions are sent to the accounts office within fourteen days of the end of the month.

An end of year summary for each employee must be filled in at the end of each tax year. All details are then recorded on one statement and sent to the tax office.

Each employee should receive a copy of form P60 at the end of each tax year. This is a summary of gross and net pay during the year.

These procedures will not have to be carried out if the employee earns less than a minimum amount, which is laid down by the tax office but they must still be informed.

When a new employee commences work they should provide a copy of the P45 which has been given by the previous employer. This is a statement of earnings and tax deducted by the previous employer. In the case of an employee not providing a P45, you must then fill in a P46 and send it to the tax office. When the employee leaves, you must provide a P45 and send a copy to the tax office.

Income tax

People of working age must fill in a tax form stating the name of their employer. Any other information relating to income, earned or unearned, must be included. A claim may be made for expenses incurred as part of the job to be set against the tax they pay. The amount of income tax paid will depend upon:

o   Income.
o   Allowances.

A tax allowance is given depending upon their status, married or single, whether they have dependent relatives living at home, the size of a mortgage, etc.

The Inland Revenue will give each employee a tax code which will inform the employer how much tax to deduct from their wages.

National insurance

National insurance contributions are paid to the Government jointly by the employer and the employee. These contributions go to:

o   The national insurance fund.
o   The national health service.
o   The redundancy fund.

Contributions pay for the following:

o   Sickness and unemployment benefit.

Fair dismissal is when:

○ The employee was made redundant.
○ The employer can prove that the employee was not qualified or unable to do the job required.
○ The employee's conduct had been unacceptable, for example:
    –Wilful destruction of equipment or property.
    –Poor attendance record.
    –Continual bad time-keeping.
    –Theft.
○ The employer has acted reasonably when dismissing the employee.

Unfair dismissal is when:

○ The employee is dismissed because she is pregnant or not allowed to return to work after maternity leave when a suitable job is available, unless the employer has five or less employees and it would not be practicable to take the employee back.
○ When the reason for dismissal is because of trade union membership or activities.
○ When the business has been transferred to a new owner and the new owner wishes to replace an employee.
○ When an employee has been improperly selected for redundancy, for example on the grounds of sex, race, religion, a married woman or a trade unionist.

When employees have a case for unfair dismissal they can take their case to *an industrial tribunal.*

An industrial tribunal is a body appointed to investigate grievances at work. The decision of the tribunal is binding on both parties. It will normally have:

○ A legally qualified chairperson.
○ An employer's representative.
○ An employee's representative.

Constructive dismissal
This is when employees resign from their job because of the unreasonable actions of their employer.

For example, if the working hours are increased without increasing the pay or expecting employees to do something that was outside the contract of employment and which they may feel to be illegal. On these grounds a tribunal may judge an employee to be unfairly dismissed.

Advisory, Conciliation and Arbitration Service (ACAS)
An employer can obtain advice from ACAS on employment practice and there are offices in most large UK cities. The conciliation service is provided to help in solving problems between employers and employees, through informal discussion.

The cases most often dealt with are of dismissed employees seeking compensation. ACAS also deals with collective issues such as pay claims or other disputes.

Conciliation is the process of trying to get each side in a dispute to appreciate the other's point of view.

Arbitration is a process through which both parties in a dispute allow a third party to reach a decision.

Employee grievance procedures

Each employee has the right to seek redress for any grievance relating to conditions of employment.

○ The matter should be raised with the employee's immediate superior and they may be accompanied by a fellow employee.
○ The matter should be dealt with without delay.
○ If the response is not satisfactory to the employee the matter may be referred higher.
○ Results of all meetings should be recorded in writing and copies given to all parties concerned.

Dealing with a grievance interview

When dealing with a grievance interview the manager is usually unable to prepare for it in advance and the employee may have been storing up the grievance for weeks so a structured framework is therefore advisable. The format for the interview should include:

Objectives
○ To obtain the facts.
○ To arrive at an acceptable solution.

Strategy
o   Aim for a mutually beneficial result.

Tactics
o   Listen to the employee's story.
o   Ask probing questions to elicit the facts.
o   Summarize from time to time to ensure mutual understanding.
o   Attempt to unravel the cause of the grievance.
o   Check the facts and meet the other parties involved.

o   Consider actions that could be taken and assess their consequences.
o   Reply to the aggrieved employee and record the actions to be taken.

Results
o   The employee should go away feeling reassured that there is no problem or that the problem has been tackled constructively.
o   The manager should feel that the grievance has been handled correctly and that both parties are satisfied.

4 Health and safety management

It is an important task for any manager to devise a health and safety policy and promote it within the business. Employees should be involved in this process and contribute by making suggestions for improvement. This should prevent accidents occurring and provide a safe environment for all members of staff and clients.

The health and safety policy

The purpose of a health and safety policy is to provide concise information for all employees about the organization's health and safety aims, objectives and how these may be achieved. In written form it is a clear guideline and will provide a record of the standards set by the management.

The following points should be included in a health and safety policy:

○ The designated responsibility of the manager.
○ The designated responsibility of supervisors.
○ The duties of employees to include statutory and the organization's own rules.
○ Systems used to monitor health and safety performance.
○ Health and safety training provided.
○ Identification of hazards and risks.
○ Fire precautions.
○ Facilities for dealing with accidents.
○ Methods of recording accidents and contravention of health and safety rules.
○ Facility for consultation with management regarding health and safety.

Statute law

This is the written law of the land and consists of Acts of Parliament and the rules and regulations which are made relating to the Acts. An Act of Parliament itself sets out the principles and objectives while the regulations are made to help in achieving these objectives. Regulations are often written into an Act of Parliament years later.

The laws relating to health and safety at work with relevance to the health and beauty salon are:

○ The Health and Safety at Work Act 1974.
○ The Management of Health and Safety at Work Regulations 1992.
○ The Offices, Shops and Railway Premises Act 1963.
○ Local Government (Miscellaneous Provisions) Act 1982.
○ The Fire Precautions Act 1971.
○ The Control of Substances Hazardous to Health Regulations 1988.
○ The Electricity at Work Regulations 1989.
○ The Health and Safety (First Aid) Regulations 1981.
○ The Reporting of Injuries, Disease and Dangerous Occurrences Regulations 1985.
○ The Safety Representatives and Safety Committees Regulations 1977.
○ Classification, Packaging and Labelling of Dangerous Substances Regulations 1984.

Bylaws

These are laws which are made at a local rather than national level and are made by the local council. A business may have to consider some of the following.

Planning permission must be sought from the local council if the present use has changed and this will include changing a shop window. The planning department and the public

TOP TO TOE HEALTH AND BEAUTY SALON
Policy on Health and Safety at Work

It is the policy of this establishment to make every reasonable and practicable effort to maintain a safe and healthy working environment for all employees and members of the public.

The establishment recognizes that the responsibility for enforcing this policy lies with the management. However, all employees must accept a joint responsibility for the safety of themselves, their colleagues and members of the public.

The co-ordination and monitoring of the safety at work policy and effective safety communication with the establishment will be the responsibility of Joan McLouglin, the elected safety representative. The management will ensure that every effort is made to meet the statutory requirements and codes of practice relating to the activities of the salon and any relevant recommendations from bodies dealing with health and safety.

To achieve this we will:
Provide training in safety procedures.
Appoint a safety representative.
Implement safe systems of work.
Provide information about specific hazards.
Issue protective clothing where possible.
Monitor safety procedures.
Provide training in fire and evacuation procedures.
Check all electrical equipment once a year.
Provide training in first aid.
Record all accidents.
Provide adequate rest facilities.
Provide a healthy environment.

Since employees are under a legal obligation to co-operate in matters of health, safety and welfare, all must accept personal responsibility for the prevention of accidents.

All employees will be informed of any revision of this policy.

A copy of the health and safety rules of the establishment are displayed in the staff room.

Karon Holmes
Proprietor

Figure 4.1 *An example of a health and safety policy*

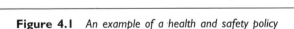

highways department will decide if the business or proposed changes will not cause aggravation to local residents or greatly affect the flow of traffic and that parking facilities are adequate.

Building regulations administered by building control officers working for the local council must be strictly adhered to, to ensure the good health and safety of the public.

Fire regulations are important and must be followed when making any structural alterations particularly if it involves a second floor or an area below ground level. A local fire officer will provide necessary advice to ensure safety, the provision of fire-fighting equipment and procedures for evacuation.

A **certification of registration** will be required when a business provides certain treatments, that is, electrical epilation, ear and body piercing and tattooing. Any person carrying out these treatments must be registered with the local authority.

Licensing is required by some local councils for certain treatment such as body massage. Licences are usually valid for one year and are granted with a set of standards and conditions for a set fee. These standards must be met or the licence may be revoked.

The Management of Health and Safety at Work Regulations 1992

The employer has certain duties according to these regulations. To:

○ Assess adequate health and safety risks to employees, clients and other members of the public who enter the premises.
○ Plan, organize and control preventative measures.
○ Monitor the preventative measures.
○ Regularly review these measures.
○ Record the results of regular services.
○ Appoint a competent person to implement evacuation procedures and to provide the necessary training.
○ Provide employees with comprehensive and relevant information regarding health and safety.
○ Provide adequate health and safety training.

The regulations also require an employer to consult with the elected safety representative (the Safety Representatives and Safety Committees Regulations 1977) in sufficient time, with issues relating to the employees represented.

These issues will include:

○ The introduction of new procedures, equipment or substances which may affect the health and safety of the employees.
○ The appointment by the employer of 'competent persons', employees who will help in assisting the employer to comply with regulations.
○ Health and safety information the employer wishes to pass on to employees.
○ Health and safety training.
○ New rulings concerning health and safety.

The Safety Representatives and Safety Committees Regulations 1977

The main objective of the regulations is to allow the appointment of a safety representative, from a trade union recognized by the employer, who will consult with the employers in matters relating to health and safety.

The number of these representatives would be in relation to:

○ The total number of employees.
○ The variety of occupations.
○ The different work activity.

A union wishing to make an appointment must apply in writing to the employer with the name of the appointed person. The safety representative may only qualify if he/she has been employed for the proceeding two years by the employer or has been employed for two years with 'similar' work experience.

The representative has the right to time off for training and to carry out the required functions of the position. The representative has the right to be consulted in sufficient time by the employer when introducing new information concerning health and safety.

Health and safety and the employee

It is of vital importance that every single employee in the business is aware of the importance of health and safety procedures and the identification of all risks and hazards.

Risk: Is the probability that harm may result from an action, situation or circumstance.
Hazard: Is the possible potential for harm to occur in a given situation.

The manager could implement a system for employees to communicate information they feel would be helpful in maintaining standards of health and safety. This could be done in three ways:

1 Regular staff meetings when health and safety matters may be discussed.
2 The facility for employees to forward any suggestions through the correct channels to the manager or owner of the business.
3 Delegate the job of monitoring health and safety in the workplace, to one member of staff, who will pass recommendations to the appropriate person.

Health and Safety at Work Act 1974

The Health and Safety at Work Act 1974 protects self-employed people and employees, with the exception of those in domestic employment in private households. The employer is responsible for ensuring that the workplace is a safe and healthy place in which to work.

If you employ five or more people you must prepare a written statement setting down the arrangements and policy you have adopted to ensure their health and safety and procedures for carrying out that policy. When employing people, therefore, it may be advisable to contact the Health and Safety Executive office in your particular area and they will advise you about your duties to your employees.

There are Inspectors of the Health and Safety Executive who have extensive powers and may enter your business premises at any reasonable time or if there is a dangerous situation. If the inspector finds a fault he/she will serve an *improvement notice*. This will state the fault and also the time which will be given to put it right. This is usually within 21 days.

A *prohibition notice* may be served, which requires the employer to stop any activity which carries risk of personal injury. If there is failure to comply with this notice then it is a criminal offence and it could lead to prosecution.

Health: Includes mental as well as physical health.

Safety: Is the freedom from foreseeable injury.

Welfare: Are the facilities available for the employee's comfort.

Employer's duties

○ To provide and maintain the place of work and systems of work that are safe and without risk to health.
○ To ensure safety when storing and using equipment and substances.
○ To provide the necessary information, instruction, training and supervision to ensure health and safety.
○ To maintain the place of work in a safe condition and without risk to health.
○ To provide and maintain the access to the place of work and all exits.
○ To provide and maintain a safe and healthy working environment.

These are the duties of the employer, so far as it is reasonably practicable. Failure to implement these duties may give rise to criminal liability and to a claim for damages.

Employees' duties

To ensure health and safety at work there must be cooperation between the employee and the employer. Employees must therefore be responsible for the health and safety of:

○ Themselves.
○ Other employees.
○ The general public.

There must be cooperation with the employer to enable the duties and requirements of the act to be carried out.

Accidents

When accidents occur they may be human or environmental.

Human error may occur through careless work, improper behaviour, lack of necessary training, unsupervised work, inexperience or fatigue.

Environmental causes of accidents may include faulty equipment, poor ventilation or poor lighting.

How to prevent accidents

The employer must be aware of any potential hazards and the possible effects on the health and safety of the workers. These hazards must then be removed:

o Entrances and exits to the premises must be kept clear.
o The premises should be well lit.
o All members of staff must be trained in the use of equipment.
o There should be no trailing leads.
o All electrical equipment should be correctly wired and well maintained.
o Power points must not be overloaded.
o Checks should be made regularly for cracked plugs and frayed wires.
o All electrical equipment must be switched off before being cleaned or repaired.
o Electrical equipment should never be touched with wet hands.
o Ensure that all containers which contain chemicals are clearly marked.

The Office, Shops and Railway Premises Act 1963

This act contains legislation which aims to provide certain minimum standards relating to the health, safety and welfare of those people working in offices, shops and railway premises. The first two categories may apply to a health and beauty therapist who is working in a salon because:

o An office can be defined as a building or part of a building which is used for administration, handling money, operating telephones and all forms of clerical work or similar activity.
o A shop will include any place of work where retail or wholesale trade is carried out. The act deals with the working environment and welfare provisions for employees.

Working environment

o The premises and all fixtures and fittings must be kept clean.
o Dirt and refuse must be removed daily.

o There must be adequate drainage.
o The number of people employed in the business must not cause a risk of injury or risk to health.
o A reasonable working temperature must be maintained not less than 16° C after the first hour.
o Effective ventilation must be provided.
o Humidity levels should be maintained.
o Fumes and dust must be controlled.
o Suitable lighting in all work areas with windows and skylights being kept clean.
o Floors passageways and stairs should be kept clear of obstruction.
o Handrails must be provided on stairs with open sides.

Ventilation

Good ventilation is essential in a salon to provide a healthy environment for employees and clients. It is a process which allows stale air to be replaced by fresh air.

Ventilation may be produced naturally through open windows or doors, the disadvantage of this method is the noise which may be evident and also lack of privacy for the client.

Artificial ventilation may be provided in several ways:

o Free-standing fans which are portable and may be utilized when and where they are required. This produces air movement but is not an efficient method of ventilation.
o A supply system which supplies fresh air from outside and filtered to remove dust.
o An exhaust system which literally pushes air outside from the salon.
o The ideal combination is the supply and exhaust system together with an air-conditioning unit.

Air conditioning

An air conditioning unit filters out particles of dust and either cools or warms the air depending on what is required and moistens or dries the air to maintain the correct humidity level.

Humidity

When humidity is high it may be uncomfortable for the client as well as the therapist. It is most important to control the humidity levels particularly when sauna, steam and other heat treatments are in use, to prevent problems occurring such as headache, fatigue and irritability.

Welfare provision

There must be a sufficient number of toilets, easily accessible, kept clean and tidy with good lighting and ventilation:

○ Up to five employees of either sex – one toilet.
○ Over five employees – one for each sex.
○ Over ten employees and if the public have access extra toilet facilities must be provided.

Other provisions to be provided include:

○ Washing facilities must be suitable and include a supply of clean hot and cold running water, soap and clean towels or another means of drying.
○ There must be a supply of clean drinking water and cups, unless provided by a water jet.
○ Facilities for rest and eating must be provided when meals are taken on the premises.
○ There must be provision for clothing particularly when the employee has to wear a uniform.
○ There must be adequate first aid facilities.
○ Adequate provision for fire prevention must be provided.

Figure 4.2 *A certificate of registration issued by a local authority*

No....*60*..

LOCAL GOVERNMENT (MISCELLANEOUS PROVISIONS) ACT 1982

Certificate of registration to carry on the [Business of [Ear-Piercing] [Electrolysis]]

THIS IS TO CERTIFY that   *KARON CHRISTINE HOLMES*

of   *14 CAPESTHORNE ROAD,   TIMPERLEY*

carrying on the [business of [ear-piercing] [electrolysis]] on the premises situated at

208 MOSS LANE, ALTRINCHAM

is duly registered in respect of such premises by the*

TRAFFORD BOROUGH COUNCIL

in accordance with the provisions of the above Act.

DATED *3rd OCTOBER*   19*94*

(Signed) ......*M S Jasper*..........................†
PRINCIPAL ENVIRONMENTAL HEALTH OFFICER
The officer appointed for this purpose.

* Insert name of local authority.   †Insert designation of proper officer

NOTE: This certificate, together with a copy of any byelaws made under the Act relating to the practice or business, must be prominently displayed on the premises. Failure to do so is an offence.

This Act has been superseded by the Health and Safety at Work Act 1974, which covers all employees.

All accidents must be recorded in an accident book, giving details of how, where and when the accident occurred, the names and addresses of the staff and clients involved and the first aid procedures carried out. Details will be required if a claim for injury benefit is made from the DSS.

Training and supervision of employees must be maintained.

Employers should prepare a written statement of their general policies concerning the health and safety of the employees if there are more than five employed.

Local Government (Miscellaneous Provisions) Act 1982

This is an important Act to any therapist who is providing electrical epilation treatments or ear-piercing. Each individual should be registered with the local authority before providing these services.

The environmental health department of the local authority will send an inspector to check that the premises are hygienic, the correct methods of sterilization are employed and the procedure to be followed in the disposal of needles is safe. When the inspector is satisfied he/she will issue a certificate.

Safe systems at work

Accidents involving members of staff and clients will be eliminated or greatly reduced if safe systems of work are put into practice. A safe system of work is the way a procedure is carried out to ensure maximum safety.

The manager can devise a safe system by:

○ Assessing the task.
○ Identifying the hazards and risk.
○ Defining a safe system.
○ Implementing the system.
○ Monitoring the system.

Task assessment

1 Write down the procedure.
2 List what equipment and products are used.
3 Look at where the procedure is carried out.
4 Look for possible sources or errors.
5 Look at how the procedure is carried out.
6 Carry out the procedure with an employee.

Identifying the hazards and risks

For each individual element of the procedure identify and record any possible hazard or risk to the client or therapist.

Defining a safe system

Once a procedure has been agreed upon and is deemed safe the information is then passed on to other members of staff, orally and in written form, with a copy safely filed away for reference.

Implementing the system

All members of staff must follow the set procedures, therefore training must be given when required and the manager is responsible for ensuring all information has been communicated to and understood by the employees.

Monitoring the system

Regular checks and staff appraisal must be made to maintain standards and information must be revised when necessary. Have regular meetings with employees to check that the systems in place are safe and working effectively.

The Health and Safety (First Aid) Regulations 1981

These regulations came into force in 1981 and they stipulate the minimum requirements for the provision of first aid at a place of work. The requirements vary depending upon the number of staff employed and the type of work which is carried out.

The following list is based on five members of staff being employed. The first aid box should be clearly labelled and contain the following:

o One guidance card.
o Ten individually wrapped sterile adhesive dressings.
o One sterile eye pad with attachment.
o One extra large sterile unmedicated dressing.
o One triangular bandage.
o One sterile covering for serious wounds.
o Six safety pins.
o Three medium-sized sterile unmedicated dressings.
o One large sterile unmedicated dressing.

There should be at least one employee who has been adequately trained in first aid. This must be brought to the attention of all members of staff as this person should be responsible for carrying out all first aid procedures and replacing any items which have been used. In the absence of that person there must be an equally qualified person to take charge of all first aid duties

Emergency phone numbers should be listed and stored in the first aid box; for example doctor, fire service, ambulance service.

The box should be stored in a dust-proof and damp-free atmosphere to keep the contents in good condition.

The employer must inform employees of all first aid arrangements including the location of equipment, facilities and the person in charge of it.

When an accident occurs the person responsible for first aid should:

o Assess the situation.
o Identify the problem.
o Provide the appropriate treatment.
o Arrange transport to the doctor or hospital if the condition so requires.

It is inevitable that even in the most safety conscious establishments accidents may occur which will require attention from a qualified member of staff. These may include:

Figure 4.3 *The recovery position*

Fainting

A temporary loss of consciousness caused by a reduced flow of blood to the brain.

Treatment
Lie the client down with legs raised slightly to stimulate the flow of blood to the brain or place in the recovery position if there is any difficulty in breathing, to maintain an open airway (see Figure 4.3). If clients only feel faint sit them down and assist them in leaning forward with their head between their knees. Loosen tight clothing, keep warm and supply fresh air.

Burns and scalds

Injuries to skin tissue, burns are caused by dry heat and scalds are caused by wet heat. A *superficial* burn causes redness, swelling and tenderness of the epidermis. Intermediate burns affect the dermis and in addition to redness and swelling will be painful and blistered.

Treatment
Cool the area immediately, preferably with cold water by immersion or holding the part under running water. Cover the area with a sterile dressing and seek medical attention if seriously burnt. Always remove rings, watches or constricting clothes from the injured area before any swelling occurs.

Blisters which occur are protective, preventing infection entering the wound therefore they must not be broken.

Chemical burns

May be caused by the acids and alkalis found in dyes, bleaches or antiseptics and disinfectants which have not been diluted. Some cleaning products may also cause a chemical burn when they come into the skin. If all safety precautions are not adhered to during galvanic treatment the concentration of acids and alkaline formed may cause a burn which penetrates deeply into the skin.

Treatment
Flush with lots of cold water, remove any clothing which may have chemicals on it and cover the area with a sterile dressing. Seek medical attention if necessary.

Electric shock

Electrical injuries may result from faulty equipment, loose wires, switches or frayed cables. Handling appliances with wet hands will increase the risk of injury

Treatment
Switch off the current at the mains or unplug the equipment. If this is not possible stand on an insulator, for example clothing, paper or rubber mat and using a wooden broom handle or chair to push the equipment or cable away from the injured person or remove their limbs from contact with the source.

If breathing is normal place the injured person in the recovery position, send for medical help and treat for shock.

Shock

May vary from a feeling of faintness to complete collapse. It may be caused by blood or fluid loss, heart attack, extreme pain, fear or electrical injury.

Treatment
Reassure and comfort the client, keep warm and loosen their clothing. Treat the cause of shock

when possible and lie the client in the recovery position if there is a possibility of vomiting.

Seek immediate medical help in severe cases.

Cuts or wounds

A cut is a break in the skin which allows blood to escape, and germs or bacteria may enter and cause infection.

Treatment
For a minor cut, clean around the wound with warm water and a mild antiseptic. Apply slight pressure over a pad of dry sterile gauze for 2–4 minutes and the bleeding should stop. Apply a clean adhesive dressing. For deep cuts seek medical assistance and try to control the bleeding by applying pressure at either side and cover with a sterile dressing once the bleeding has stopped. Use disposable plastic gloves if possible.

Eye injuries

These include a foreign body or chemicals in the eye.

Treatment
Chemicals may be washed out with a large amount of cold water. A foreign body may be removed by using a twisted, moistened corner of a sterile dressing or bathing the eye using an eyebath and lukewarm water. Seek medical attention in more severe cases.

Asthmatic attack

Caused by the muscles of the air passages going into spasm making breathing very difficult. Asthma may be triggered by an allergy or nervous tension and the condition is controlled by the sufferer with medication.

Treatment
Reassure and calm the client, sit them up in a comfortable position leaning on the back of a chair or table. Loosen the clothing and ensure a good supply of fresh air. Make sure clients take their medication if it is available.

Seek medical attention in severe cases.

Fire regulations

The Fire Precautions Act 1971 is concerned with fire prevention and the provision of fire escapes. A fire certificate is required if:

o There are more than twenty people employed at any time.
o There are more than ten people working anywhere other than the ground floor.
o When the total number of people working in the building, including the salon, exceeds twenty.

Employers have a duty to provide a means of escape in case of fire for both their employees and any members of the public on the premises at the time.

Once a certificate has been granted it must be kept on the premises as long as it is in force and it will state:

o The greatest number of people who can safely be employed at any one time on the premises.
o The means of escape to be used.
o The exits to be marked as fire escapes.
o Any special risks in the structure of the premises.

Employers must ensure that any means of escape will be kept clear of obstruction at all times, kept in good working order and doors must be unlocked. All employees must be made aware of the means of escape and the procedures to be followed in case of fire.

The fire-fighting equipment suitable for all types of fire including chemical and electrical must be easily reached and kept in good working order.

Any breach of the fire regulations could make you liable for a fine or imprisonment.

Fire extinguishers

Fire extinguishers are colour coded and there are five different types which are used for different types of fire:

Powder

Blue in colour for flammable liquids, gases and electrical equipment. This may cause sensitivity if it comes into contact with the skin.

CO_2 gas

Black in colour for flammable liquids, gases and electrical equipment.

These two extinguishers may be used in a beauty salon where electrical equipment is used. Both types of extinguisher have limited cooling properties therefore it is advisable to use a fire blanket after the extinguisher, to deprive the fire of oxygen and prevent re-ignition.

Water

Red in colour for wood, paper, textiles, fabric and similar material. It must never be used on burning liquid, electrical or flammable metal fires.

Foam

Yellow in colour and may be used on burning liquid fires. It must never be used on electrical or flammable metal fires.

Halon

Green in colour for burning liquid fires. It must not be used on flammable metal fires.

Precautions

The fire extinguisher may be used on a small fire but in the event of a serious fire, it is important to evacuate the premises as quickly as possible.

Do not attempt to retrieve personal belongings.

Guide your client or employees for whom you are responsible, to the nearest fire exit, closing the doors behind you.

(a) A *water* extinguisher for use on paper, wood textiles, and fabric. It must not be used on burning liquid, electrical or flammable metal fires

(b) A *foam* extinguisher for use on burning liquid fires. It must not be used on electrical or flammable metal fires

(c) A *powder* extinguisher for use on burning liquid and electrical fires. It must not be used on flammable metal fires

(d) A *halon* extinguisher for use on burning liquid and electrical fires. It must not be used on flammable metal fires

(e) A *carbon dioxide* extinguisher for use on burning liquid and electrical fires. It must not be used on flammable metal fires

(f) A light-duty *fire* blanket for use on burning liquids and burning cloth. Heavy-duty fire blankets are available for industrial use

Figure 4.4   *Types of fire extinguisher*

Ring the emergency services by dialling 999 and provide the necessary information:

○   Location of the fire and address.
○   The nature of the fire.

The Electricity at Work Regulations 1989

These regulations are concerned with ensuring safety when using electrical equipment. The management have responsibility to ensure:

○   All electrical equipment is properly maintained and in good working order.
○   Regular tests are made by a qualified electrician on each piece of equipment – at least once a year.
○   A record of each test and the date the tests were carried out is made and provided for inspection if necessary.

It is the responsibility of all employees to co-operate with their employer in complying with the regulations. A set of rules may be devised by the manager to inform each employee of their daily responsibilities in maintaining electrical equipment in good working order:

o Store equipment safely in its designated place with all the wires and attachments securely fixed in place.
o Clean equipment after each use.
o Place the equipment on a stable surface when in use.
o Check the wires are not twisted, worn or frayed.
o Check the plug has the correct fuse.
o Check the plug is not cracked or loose.
o Do not overload plug sockets by using multiple adaptors.
o Ensure there are no trailing leads which someone could fall over.
o Always dry your hands before touching the plug or equipment.
o Do not place equipment on or near water.
o Always follow the manufacturer's instructions.
o Report faulty equipment to your superior and store it safely to be repaired.

Control of Substances Hazardous to Health Act 1989

There are products used by beauty therapists that may be hazardous to health if they are not stored and used correctly, following procedures laid down by the organization. The health and safety welfare, of all employees and members of the public with access to the premises, is the responsibility of the employer by law. The manager or delegated employee (health and safety representative) has to:

o List all substances which may be hazardous to health.
o Evaluate the risks to health.
o Decide what action needs to be taken to reduce the risks.
o Devise rules and regulations about safe storage, handling, use, transportation and disposal of hazardous substances.
o Provide training for all staff in their use.

o Monitor the effectiveness of the control measures.
o Keep records up to date of all measures taken and safety checks made.

Assessment procedures

The first step is to check everything which comes into the premises, products used during practical procedures as well as products required for other services such as cleaning and sterilization.

The law requires suppliers to provide information about the safe use of the products they are selling on clearly marked labels. To recognize substances which may be hazardous it is important to read the labels carefully but do not rely solely on this information.

Check carefully what the hazards may be, do they:

o Cause irritation.
o Burn the skin.
o Give off fumes.
o Cause breathing difficulties.
o Cause allergies.

It is also useful to research information from other sources which may be of help. These could include:

o Other therapists.
o Health and safety experts.
o Company representatives.
o Manufacturers.
o Professional trade organizations.

Obtaining all published material concerning health and safety, available from health and safety executive public enquiry points:

Health and Safety
Executive,
Broad Lane,
Sheffield,
S3 7HQ
Tel: 0114 289 2345

Health and Safety
Executive,
Rose Court,
Southwark Bridge Road,
London SE1 9HF
Tel: 0171 717 6000

Labelling

Once the hazardous substances have been identified warning symbols should be applied in a prominent position according to the Classification, Packaging and Labelling of Dangerous Substances Regulations 1984.

These dangerous substances may be categorized in different ways. In relation to health and safety this will be according to the harm they can cause. Reaction may be immediately after exposure, this is an acute effect, but there are other substances which have long-term effects on the body only after repeated exposure, and this is known as a chronic effect.

Classification

Corrosives: These are substances which attack chemically, materials or people.

Explosive and flammable: These are dangerous because of the rapid release of energy and the harm that they cause as a result of combustion.

Harmful: These substances present a limited risk to health if inhaled, ingested or enter the body through the skin.

Irritants: These will have a detrimental affect on the skin or respiratory tract.

Oxidizing: These are substances which give off heat when they come into contact with other substances, in particular flammable ones.

Toxics: These are substances which prevent or interfere with body functions in a variety of ways.

All therapists must be aware of the potential risk involved when handling hazardous substances in the course of their work.

Storage

Any product which has been identified as hazardous must be stored in a cool, dry place, with good ventilation away from direct sunlight. A metal cupboard with adjustable shelving is ideal for flammable products and large heavy items must be stored on the low shelves and always resealed after each use.

Handling

All treatment rooms should have good ventilation to remove fumes and freshen the air.

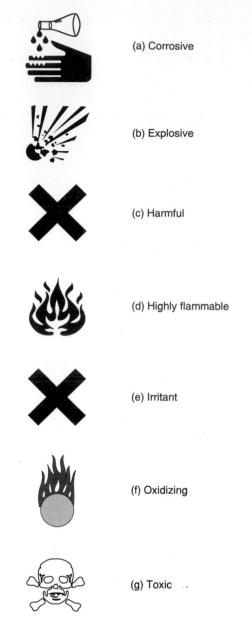

(a) Corrosive

(b) Explosive

(c) Harmful

(d) Highly flammable

(e) Irritant

(f) Oxidizing

(g) Toxic

Figure 4.5 *Classification of hazardous substances*

Therapists must wear protective clothing when using substances which may cause harm. Gloves may be used to protect the hands particularly when using cleaning fluids. Masks may be worn to prevent inhalation of fine powder and goggles to protect the eyes from irritation.

ACCIDENT REPORT FORM

Date: Time of Accident:

Name:	Age:
Address:	
Relationship to salon:	
Nature of visit to salon:	Contact Tel No:

Brief description of Accident:

_____

Location of accident:

_____

Cause of accident (list all materials used):

_____

_____

Damage incurred to injured person:

_____

Action Taken:

_____

_____

Witnesses:

Signature of Client: Date

Signature of Witnesses: Date:

                                Date:

Signature of Therapist: Date:

Signature of Manager: Date:

Figure 4.6 *An example of an accident report form*

Smoking must be prohibited when handling any hazardous substance.

Always ensure the manufacturer's instructions are strictly adhered to at all times, particularly in the dilution of concentrated substances.

Aerosol sprays must be kept cool and away from heat while in use and must never be sprayed near a naked flame.

The Reporting of Injuries, Diseases and Dangerous Occurrences Regulations 1985

These regulations cover all employees, clients or members of the public who suffer injury or a condition resulting from a work activity.

The purpose of these regulations is to ensure the information regarding incidents or injury arising from work activities is provided to the enforcing authority by the person responsible within the organization.

To prevent any future accidents or injury occurring the information is useful to highlight areas which require improvement or change in practice.

The procedure

o   The relevant enforcing authority should be contacted immediately regarding injury, disease or a dangerous occurrence which results from work activities. The enforcing authority will be the Health and Safety Executive or local authority.
o   The person to provide the information would be the manager or the person who has been given the responsibility within the organization for the control of health and safety.
o   Information could be transmitted immediately by telephone and then a written report with all the details should be sent within seven days.
o   Form F2508 must be used when reporting injuries and dangerous occurrences.
o   Form F2508A must be used when reporting disease only if there is written confirmation from a medical practitioner that the disease is listed and is a result of work activity.
o   Records must be kept and can be entered into the accident book, Form B1510 and photocopies of any reports sent to the enforcing authority. These records should be kept for a minimum of three years from the date they were made.

Manual Handling Operations Regulations 1992

These regulations have been introduced under the provisions of the Health and Safety at Work Act. They implement the requirements of a European directive on the manual handling of loads, to prevent injury from moving or lifting heavy objects by hand or bodily force. The most common injuries are sprains and strains, often to the back, due to incorrect methods of lifting and handling or prolonged use of body force.

Many injuries which occur are cumulative rather than being caused by one single incident. Therefore, the employer is required to assess any task which involves manual handling of loads and take into account:

o   The task to be undertaken.
o   The capabilities of the staff.
o   The limitations of the staff.
o   The type of load to be handled.
o   The working environment.

Risk of injury may be avoided

o   By eliminating the need to manually handle any heavy load, e.g. repair heavy equipment *in situ* and arrange for heavy goods to be delivered to the point of use.
o   By handling heavy loads by other means such as automation, a power system and using trolleys for transportation.
o   By training all members of staff in correct procedures when handling heavy loads, making loads smaller, lighter or easier to grasp.

The duties of the employee are

o   To take reasonable care for their own health and safety and others who may be affected by their activities.
o   To co-operate with their employers to enable them to comply with their health and safety duties.
o   To make use of appropriate equipment provided for them for the safe handling of loads.
o   To follow appropriate safe systems of work laid down by the employer to promote safety during the handling of loads.

The Provision and Use of Work Equipment Regulations 1992

These regulations require that all equipment used in a salon must be suitable for the purpose for which it is used. It must also be properly maintained and all members of staff must be trained in its use. These regulations apply to any equipment whether it is new or has been bought second hand.

To comply with these regulations you must:

o   Have all equipment regularly serviced.
o   Keep records of when equipment has been checked or repaired.
o   Always check that equipment bought second hand is checked by your own service engineer or electrician.
o   Train all new members of staff in the use of equipment.
o   Have training days to update information or to evaluate use of equipment.
o   Provide written instructions in addition to training if and when required.

The Personal Protective Equipment at Work Regulations 1992

These regulations require every employer to provide protective equipment to any employee who may be exposed to any risk to health or injury during working hours.

To comply with these regulations:

o   Assess the need for use of personal protective equipment.
o   Supply protective clothing or equipment free of charge.
o   Train staff in use of personal protective equipment.
o   Ensure all such equipment is well maintained.
o   Ensure it is suitable for the nature of the work.

The Health and Safety (Display Screen Equipment) Regulations 1992

With the increasing use of computers in all types of business these regulations must be complied with if any employees are using equipment which may cause the following:

o   Eye strain.
o   Mental stress.
o   Muscular pain.
o   Other physical problems.

The duty of the employer is to:

o   Assess the equipment and the work station for risk of injury or strain to the employee.
o   Plan the display screen equipment so that there are breaks or changes of activity.
o   Provide training for the employees using the equipment.
o   Provide any special spectacles needed but they must be paid for by the employer.
o   Provide a properly designed desk and chair.

The Environmental Protection Act 1990

This Act is relevant to the hair and beauty industry in that some products used may contain hazardous substances which must be disposed of safely.

Any person disposing of 'waste' has a duty to dispose of it safely in such a way that it does not cause harm to the environment or individual.

There are occasions when out-of-date stock must be disposed of and it may be necessary to consult with the manufacturer for advice. To comply with this Act:

o   Obtain the relevant information from suppliers about the safe use and disposal of products.
o   Provide training for all employees in the safe disposal of products or chemicals.
o   Never dispose of chemical products where they may be found by any unauthorized person, in particular, children.

5 Marketing

The market may be defined as a group of existing clients and potential clients who will use your services and products.

A very important function in any business is to increase turnover and profits. Marketing, therefore, is a key managerial function, particularly in the health and beauty business which is so highly customer-orientated. It is essential to:

○ Assess clients' needs and wants.
○ Monitor changes in the market place.
○ Anticipate future trends.
○ Promote the business.

Marketing is an ongoing process or business philosophy which helps to provide what the client needs and wants and allows a business to be prepared to respond to change. Marketing activities will include:

○ Creating the right image.
○ Market research.
○ Testing products on consumers.
○ Advertising.
○ Selling.
○ Promotions.

The importance of marketing as a managerial function for beauty and hairdressing salons has increased over the last forty years for several reasons:

Economic growth: There has been an increase in the disposable income of many consumers and this has resulted in a growth in demand for products and services in a far wider range of choice.

Fashion: There has been a considerable change in fashion, taste and lifestyle of consumers. Many more women consider a visit to the hairdresser or beauty therapist a necessity rather than a luxury and men are becoming increasingly more aware of the therapeutic treatments that are available.

Technology: Firms are constantly inventing, designing and launching new or more advanced products onto the market offering increased benefits to the consumer

Competition: The number of businesses competing for the consumer's attention is constantly increasing therefore marketing is vital to each business in maintaining its market share.

The marketing mix

To achieve marketing objectives a business must consider the 'marketing mix':

PRODUCT PRICE PLACE PROMOTION

To meet consumer needs the business must produce the right *product* at the right *price*, make it available in the right *place* and let the consumers know about it through *promotion*.

Market research

To be successful, the services you offer and the product you sell must meet the requirements of your clientele. Therefore, efficient market research is vital.

There are several methods of evaluating the needs of your clients:

1 Talk to your clients when you have their initial consultation and complete their record card. They will give you a clear indication of their beauty needs and you can ask them certain pertinent questions to elicit the information you require.

2 Listen to your clients. They may have a specific request or they may casually mention a new product or service that they are interested in while they are waiting for treatment. Discussions may occur naturally during treatment as a result of a query they have made or advice you may be giving.

3   Compile a questionnaire that you can send to all existing clients with relevant questions about the services you are already offering and new services you are proposing. You may then assess the likely response to the introduction of new treatments and whether it is a worthwhile investment.

4   Attend professional health and beauty shows, held nationally or internationally, to provide you with the most up-to-date information about services, treatments, trends and products. Many companies use these exhibitions to launch their latest and most up-to-date procedures and treatments and you have the opportunity to compare different companies together.

5   Subscribe to professional health and beauty publications as they will provide addresses, telephone numbers of many companies as well as articles and information which will keep you abreast of current trends. They also provide an efficient service allowing you to receive all the information you require from the companies of your choice, by filling in one reference card and sending this to them directly to process. This saves you time and the expense of contacting individual companies yourself.

Market orientation

A market-orientated business is one which continually identifies, reviews and analyses consumer needs. This is particularly important in a highly competitive industry which is so customer-orientated. It will allow the business to:

o   Anticipate market changes.
o   Respond more quickly to these changes.
o   Be in a stronger position to meet the challenge.
o   Be more confident of success when launching new treatments or products.
o   Ensure the requirements of the consumer are identified, can be met and are constantly reviewed.

Consumer categories

Consumers, purchasers and clients all differ in terms of income, attitude and preferences. They all have different priorities and may be categorized according to their socio-economic group:

o   Young singles.
o   Young marrieds with no children.
o   Young marrieds with youngest child under six.
o   Young marrieds with youngest child over six.
o   Older marrieds with children under eighteen.
o   Older marrieds with no children under eighteen.
o   Older singles.
o   Others.

Each of these groups will have different amounts of disposable income and different priorities. Some may be restricted by their working hours, looking after children or a lack of mobility. Conversely, they may have an abundance of time. They will all require different services, treatments and products and will therefore respond to different marketing methods.

The psychological factor is also important in marketing health and beauty therapy products as appeals may be made to conflicting motivations. Emphasis may be placed on the benefits to health, from particular treatments which provide an antidote to the stresses and strains of modern life. At the more expensive end of the market and particularly when selling skin care and makeup products, emphasis may be placed on the exclusiveness or distinctiveness of a particular line. Advertising could also be aimed at a large segment of the market, taking advantage of the need to belong to a group, the group may be associated with a particular lifestyle, concept or moral stance. Consumers may be strong supporters of 'beauty without cruelty', buying only products which are not tested on animals or contain animal by-products or treatments which imply exclusivity and wealth reflecting a lifestyle to which they aspire.

Marketing therefore takes into account people's need to fulfil their various roles and aspirations.

The product

In any health and beauty establishment the 'product' means the services offered and the retail lines available to buy. There are many different types of treatments available, covering a wide range and this is called a product mix.

In a typical salon this 'product mix' could include:

○ Facial therapy.
○ Body therapy.
○ Hand, foot and nail treatments.
○ Holistic therapy.

Within most of these product lines variety may be offered, for example:

Facial therapy

○ Basic manual treatments.
○ Specialized electrical treatments.
○ Anti-ageing treatments.
○ Eye treatments.
○ Permanent makeup.

Body therapy

○ Electrical slimming treatments.
○ Body wrapping.
○ Anti-cellulite treatment.
○ Body brushing.
○ Spot reduction.
○ Body toning.
○ Heat therapy.

Hand, foot and nail treatments

○ Manicure.
○ Pedicure.
○ Nail extensions.
○ Natural nail cultivation.
○ Depilatory waxing.

Holistic therapy

○ Aromatherapy.
○ Reflexology.
○ Shiatsu.
○ Iridology.

Clients will buy the product which provides the greatest benefit to them, no matter what features the product has. Therefore, when promoting products, emphasis must be placed upon what the end result will be in having a particular treatment or buying a particular product.

There are many companies selling their particular treatments and products for professional and retail use. To provide the appropriate products for your own clientele there are several considerations.

Brand names

Choosing a well-known brand name has the advantage that many people will be familiar with the product. The business will benefit from any advertising, which will probably be on a national level, that the company carries out. Some brand names are synonymous with a particular image concept or quality which would be applied to the business if the branded product is used.

Packaging

The presentation of a product to clients is very important because, no matter how good the benefits of a product are, if it is unappealing to look at they will probably look for an alternative elsewhere. The look of a product particularly in retail skin care, body care and makeup reinforces the brand image, for example, the neutral colours of recycled packaging which may be used by a company who holds environmental issues as a high priority or the sophisticated black and gold packaging of the company promoting glamour. The packaging also provides point of sale attraction to a potential customer who may then consider the benefits of the product or be persuaded to buy.

Packaging must also be functional as it protects some items such as glass bottles from breakage and may be see-through to allow the customer to see the product quickly and easily while maintaining the quality of the outer packaging due to less handling.

Variety

It is necessary to provide a variety of treatments and products to maintain client interest. The variety chosen must be appropriate to the market, the treatments should be introduced only when they are required, as investing money in stock or equipment which are not used is wasted capital. When buying retail products it is advisable to buy from a company who provides variety, does not require a minimum order and will deliver quickly.

Quality

Aiming for quality of treatments, products and services is an essential ingredient in business success. Time taken to research companies is well spent if the end result produces a quality product. Make sure that equipment is tried and tested before agreeing to buy, you may then see and feel the quality for yourself. Samples of products you intend to purchase should be provided so that an informed decision can be made.

The life cycle of a product

Trends in treatments and services have changed greatly in the beauty industry over the last ten years. Emphasis has changed often from one aspect to another highlighting the life cycle of a product. Several years ago there was a boom in the use of sun beds and solaria to produce an all-year round golden tan. Research in recent years has shown that the exposure to any form of ultra-violet radiation is harmful to the skin in that it may cause cancer and premature ageing and these facts have been constantly reinforced through the media, in magazines, newspapers and on television, as well as from the medical profession.

The increased awareness of the general public to these dangers and their insistence on using a different safer method to produce a tan has provided the opportunity for therapists to offer a fake tan treatment. This service is now growing rapidly to satisfy the demand while the use of sun beds is declining. There may be many other factors which will contribute to the growth or decline in a particular product or treatment, such as:

Growth of a product

○ It is fashionable.
○ Well-promoted creating a demand.
○ High-quality product.
○ Improves the quality of life.
○ Promotes good health.
○ Has noticeable benefits.
○ Environmentally friendly.
○ Therapeutic.

Decline of a product

○ Saturation in the market place.
○ It is unfashionable.
○ Proved to be ineffective.
○ Does not live up to expectations.
○ Cost is prohibitive.
○ Not environmentally friendly.

A good manager will be aware of problems which arise at each stage in the product life cycle and take the necessary measures to cope.

Stages of the product life cycle

The introduction stage: When introducing a new treatment, the initial cost is high and sales are low so steps must be taken to promote the product and recoup the cost quickly. Offering discount on courses of new treatments booked and paid for in advance will bring in capital and ease the financial burden. The manufacturer may allow payment in instalments over a period but this may increase the overall cost of the product.

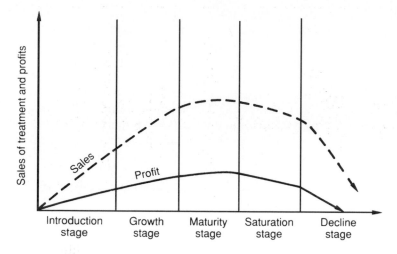

Figure 5.1 *Product/treatment life cycle*

The growth stage: The treatment is well-established and sales rise rapidly increasing profits. Capitalize on this by ensuring that there are sufficient number of staff to cope with the demand and opening hours are flexible to accommodate all clients.

The maturity stage: Sales will continue to rise but competition within the market place may cause a reduction in price of the treatment thus reducing profits.

The saturation stage: The competition is extensive, prices will fall and therefore profits will be less. Consider change or improving current treatment.

The decline stage: Sales are poor and profits low or non-existent.

A good manager will predict the correct time to change direction or improve the existing product before it goes into decline.

Promoting treatments and products

Sales promotion is a form of indirect advertising which provides incentives to stimulate sales and is used for the following reasons:

○ To draw the client's attention to a new treatment or product.

○ To stimulate sales of slow-moving lines.
○ To encourage bookings during off-peak time.
○ To increase turnover.

Types of promotion

○ Introducing a new treatment at a special introductory price for a limited period.
○ Booking a course of treatments at a discount.
○ Providing a free gift with a purchase.
○ Including a discount voucher in a newspaper advertisement or article.
○ Providing treatment packages, for example in the summer, after Christmas or a Mother's day special.

Promotions may be:

○ Used on a regular basis, for example promotion of the month. This will generate sales and allow regular clients to take advantage of special offers.
○ Timed to take advantage of seasonal trends, for example a holiday package.
○ Timed to increase turnover during quiet trading periods.
○ Aimed at particular age groups to increase client numbers.
○ Used to introduce a new service or product, for example bridal service or specialist treatments such as reflexology or sports massage.

Top to Toe

Beauty Salon
&
Toning Table Studio

208 Moss Lane
Altrincham
Cheshire
WA15 8AZ
Telephone: 0161 980 3889

Easy Parking

Karon C. Holmes I.H.B.C.C.G.L.I.
A Member of BABTAC

I am professionally trained by the International Health and Beauty Council and by the City and Guilds London Institute for Beauty Therapy and Electrolysis.

The salon offers a wide range of Beauty and Body Toning treatments in a friendly and informal atmosphere.

For your personal protection the highest standards of hygiene are observed and paramount importance is placed upon sterilisation.

For further information or advice you can telephone any time without obligation.

I look forward to meeting you.

Karon

OPENING TIMES

Monday	9.30 am to 7.30 pm
Tuesday	9.30 am to 9.00 pm
Wednesday	9.30 am to 7.30 pm
Thursday	9.30 am to 9.00 pm
Friday	9.30 am to 7.30 pm
Saturday	9.30 am to 1.00 pm

BEAUTY PROGRAMMES

Top to Toe HOLIDAY SPECIAL
HALF LEG WAX
BIKINI AND UNDER ARM WAX
LASH AND BROW TINT, BROW SHAPE
MANICURE & PEDICURE £35.00

Top to Toe RELAXING SPECIAL
MANICURE & PEDICURE
½ hour FACIAL
BACK AND NECK MASSAGE £30.00

WEDDING SPECIAL
GALVADERM FACIAL
recommended at least 10 days before
½ hour FACIAL WITH PRACTICE MAKE-UP
FRENCH MANICURE
MAKE-UP on the big day £65.00

MAKE-UP
CLEANSE AND MAKE-UP £11.00

EAR PIERCING £6.00

Gift Vouchers Available

Figure 5.2 *An example of a price list and promotions leaflet*

Figure 5.3 *An example of a salon advertisement placed in a local newspaper*

Newspapers

Most areas have a free paper which is delivered to everybody in a particular area. Therefore, the paper will probably reach more of the market than an advertisement placed in a paper which is bought only by a percentage of the population in that area.

Features, contributed by experts, are gratefully welcomed by the publishers of free papers, so that they are not just full of adverts. So

contact the editor and offer to write articles or an advice column related to your business. This will then give you valuable free advertising.

Although newspapers will often have the facility to design an advertisement for you, it may be advisable to use a professionally designed advert to catch the reader's eye. The only drawback to this is the cost of the services of a graphic designer.

A good advertisement should draw attention to the services or products you are trying to sell and be easily understood. It should convince the reader of the benefits and create a desire to either go and buy the product or sample the treatments advertised.

An interesting story about yourself, your business or somebody working for you, particularly if it is accompanied by an unusual photograph, may be deemed by a newspaper editor to be worth including in the publication. This sort of free advertising is often worth far more than a written advertisement because the general public find the objectivity of a journalist far more credible than an ad.

National newspapers would not be the right media to advertise treatment packages but would be ideal if you had a product to sell through mail order, for example your own brand of skin care products.

Local radio

It could prove quite expensive to advertise on local radio. However, your advisory services could be offered and when the occasion requires asking someone with beauty therapy experience to take part in a discussion or current affairs programme, you may be called upon and the resulting exposure could prove to be an invaluable free source of advertising.

Magazines

Placing an advertisement in the advertising section of a magazine which specializes in beauty will ensure that the people who are going to read the advert will be those most interested in the services you are offering. Because there will be other similar advertisements it is important to

Top to Toe

Beauty Salon & Toning Table Studio

For all beauty treatments toning tables, sunbeds & gift vouchers. Holiday Special, Half leg wax, bikini and under arm wax, lash and brow tint, brow shape, manicure and pedicure

208 Moss Lane, Hale, Cheshire
Tel: (0161) 980 3889

Figure 5.4 *An advertisement included in a travel agent's portfolio*

ensure that yours will be designed in such a way that it will stand out from the rest.

Specialist brochures

This can be a certain way to ensure that the target audience are all interested in the treatments advertised. An excellent example of this is the *Bridal brochure* that many large hotels produce. These brochures detail the services that they offer, as a hotel, mainly in connection with the catering and entertainment facilities they have to offer a couple who are planning a wedding. They will then invite other businesses such as florists, hairdressers and beauty salons to place advertisements in the brochure. The wedding makeup or pre-wedding beauty package could receive an excellent response, when advertised in this type of publication. Many brides who do not normally have beauty treatments will on such a special occasion. This provides you with the opportunity of gaining new business on a permanent basis, if the bride is sufficiently impressed with your work.

Leaflets/posters

Advertising leaflets can look like a second rate form of advertising unless they are of a high quality. They can be used in several ways:

○ Picked up by established clients and passed on to potential clients.
○ Given to someone who calls in to enquire about the services offered.
○ Sent out in mail shots.
○ Posted through letter boxes.
○ Given out at exhibitions or demonstrations.
○ Leaving the leaflets at another business which complements your own, for example a hairdressing salon. This could be reciprocated and their advertising literature could be left at your salon.

Posters are effective when placed in a position where they will be read by either a captive audience or where there is a considerable amount of passing trade.

An antenatal clinic has a captive audience and there are many pregnant women who may not have considered beauty treatments previously but who may now have a great need for the services of a beauty therapist, both before and after the birth of her child. She may require pedicures, waxing treatments or even a relaxing facial before the birth and she will almost certainly require help and advice after the birth, on losing weight and regaining her figure.

A poster in a busy local shop such as a newsagents or a chemist will probably be seen by a large number of people and even if the return on this form of advertising is small the value for money is excellent as it is not an expensive form of advertising.

Mail shots

By keeping a record of the addresses of all clients and any person who may have requested information from you, or names passed on through personal contact, a mailing list can be built up. This may then be used to provide information about new products or techniques and seasonal or special offers.

Word of mouth

This is a very valuable form of advertising. Once you have established a reputation for quality, professionalism and good client care and the treatments you offer are competitively priced,

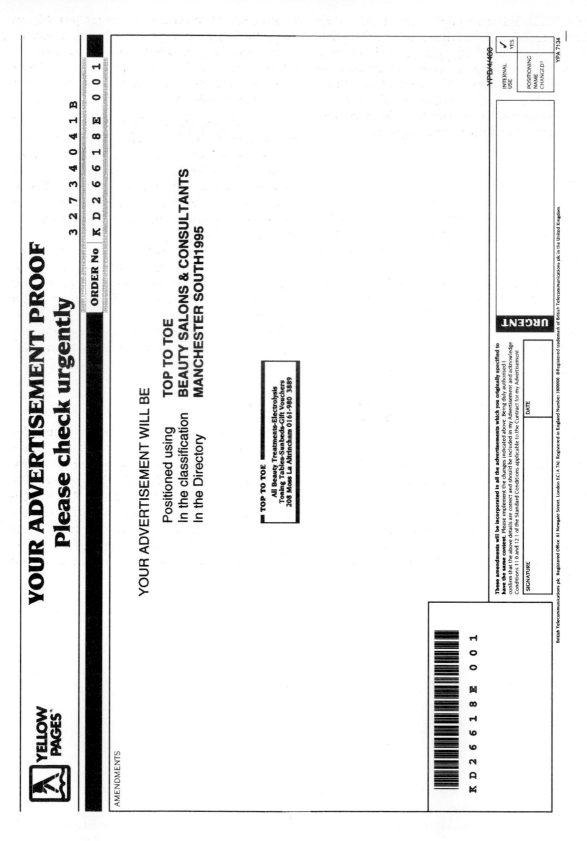

Figure 5.5 *An advertisement from Yellow Pages*

clients will automatically recommend your business to friends, relatives and colleagues, enabling you to build up your client base quite quickly. Having business cards with an address and telephone number available at all times provides a form of advertising but also ensures that a prospective client will be able to contact you even after some time has elapsed.

Demonstrations

A demonstration is an ideal way to bring a new concept or technique to the notice of the general public, or to provide a means of raising money for a charity, which will in turn provide your business with publicity. It is an interesting way of educating the public about health and beauty and promoting your own treatments in an entertaining way.

For a successful demonstration:

o Find out the type of audience and the general age group that will attend.
o Be sure of the numbers attending so that you can provide everybody with the necessary advertising literature or information leaflets, samples etc.
o Have a basic format to follow and time the demonstration well – not too long or the audience may lose interest.
o Prepare a set of cards with key points to ensure everything of importance is covered.
o Know your subject well and prepare answers to questions that you think may arise.

o Involve the audience whenever possible, in particular, encourage them to ask questions and use them as demonstration models.
o Know the retail prices of products and treatments and the advantages they have over your competitors.

Use good judgement when choosing a model from the audience, for a makeup demonstration; choose someone who will enhance your products, for example an unmade up face will show a greater difference after the application of makeup and time will not be wasted cleansing when the purpose of the demonstration is the application of makeup.

You may feel it is advisable to provide your own model to ensure that unknown factors do not interfere with the demonstration, for example a very sensitive skin or skin blemishes.

Practice the demonstration in advance if it is your first, or the particular technique being used is a new one.

Directory

Finally entering the name, address and telephone number in a directory such as *Yellow Pages* is a useful form of advertising. Many people who are looking for a service may automatically refer to a directory. It is important, therefore, when choosing a name for the business to consider choosing one which begins with one of the first letters in the alphabet so that your name is one of the first that they call.

6 *Financial management*

The purpose of any business is to make a profit by managing the financial resources effectively. Financial control is concerned with cash flow and all financial transactions should be recorded, for several reasons:

1　To provide information to the Inland Revenue.
2　To provide information to shareholders.
3　To assess business performance.
4　To help plan for the future.
5　To help improve the running of the business.
6　To control money flowing in and out of the business.
7　To prove creditworthiness to suppliers.
8　To obtain loans.

The three documents which are essential to providing an accurate plan are:

1　The balance sheet.
2　The profit and loss account.
3　The cashflow forecast.

Together these three documents provide:

○　An overview of the money in the business.
○　Where the money came from.
○　How it is invested.
○　How the business has performed.
○　How cash is managed now.
○　How cash will be managed in the future.

To prepare a balance sheet information must be provided about the following:

Funds: These may be in the form of a loan, share capital in a limited company or investment capital.
Fixed assets: These are resources acquired to help the business function, for example in a hairdressing salon they would include chairs, mirrors, back washes, dryers and other fixtures and fittings as well as the premises themselves.
Current assets: These are part of the working capital of the business and will include cash and stock.

Current liabilities: Money which is owed to creditors, bank loans and income tax.

The profit and loss account is a summary of all trading transactions in one year and it shows how financially successful the business is. It shows the net profit after tax by subtracting business expenses and taxation from the turnover.

Cashflow

Poor cashflow will cause problems for a business as cash is needed to buy resources which are used for services or goods to be bought by the client for cash.

Cash
↓
Buy stock, labour equipment, etc.
↓
Provides a service and goods for sale
↓
Goods and services sold for cash
↓
Cash received

Figure 6.1　*Cashflow*

The amount of money required to pay for the day-to-day running of the business is known as *working capital*.

Cashflow problems may be caused by:

Stockpiling: Money tied up in stock is unproductive and the minimum amount of stock should be maintained to provide an effective service. Stock control therefore is an important feature of cash management.
Spending: Large amounts of capital spent on equipment will stretch financial resources to the limit. Leasing instead of buying will leave more cash for working capital.

Over borrowing: Borrowing money for expansion will increase the amount of interest to be paid and place an added financial burden on the business.

Change in demand: Changes in fashion may cause a fall in demand for particular treatments which may lead to poor sales and less cash flowing into the business.

Seasonal changes: Business may be quiet at certain periods of the year, for example January and February after the Christmas rush or July and August when people are away.

There will inevitably be times when a business may run short of cash and when this happens the main aim is to cover costs rather than make a profit. The following steps may be taken to improve cash flow:

○ Stimulate sales by offering discounts.
○ Sell off stock at cost price or below if necessary.
○ Sell any fixed assets which are rarely used or not vital to the business.
○ Sell equipment and lease instead.
○ Think twice before making any purchases, ensure they are essential.
○ Adjust salon opening hours to meet demand.
○ Extend credit with suppliers.
○ Contact clients whose attendance may have lapsed.
○ Motivate staff to generate new business by offering incentives.
○ Use a supplier who will deliver stock quickly allowing you to maintain a low level of stock.
○ Ensure all members of staff are used effectively to increase productivity.
○ Train staff in new techniques and skills.
○ Make use of those members of staff who wish to work part-time employing them at busy times only.

Budgeting

A budget is a plan based on the objectives of a business, it will show what money is required and how it will be raised. A budget may be set for a 12 month accounting period but if necessary it can be as little as one month. A flexible budget is sometimes required to change as a business changes, for example if there is a sudden increase in demand for a particular service or treatment this will result in much higher sales levels. Therefore, the sales budget may need to be altered.

Preparation of a budget

○ Determine how long the budget period will be and decide what the objectives are.
○ Information must be collected based on results previously achieved and estimates of future sales.
○ Targets for sales must be set.

The sales budget: This contains monthly sales estimates, that is, how many treatments and products will be sold.

The production budget: This shows what the required labour hours will be, the consumables required and equipment needed to provide the services.

The main objective is to make a profit so the income from sales should cover the production cost and provide a healthy profit.

The advantages of using a budget are:

○ It helps to control income and expenditure.
○ It will draw attention to waste.
○ It provides employees with an awareness of costs.
○ It ensures that capital is used effectively.

Banking services

Commercial banks provide different services:

○ They receive money on deposit from customers providing a safe place to keep their money.
○ They lend money to the customer.
○ They transfer money for the customer to other people.

Commercial banks use the money deposited with them to provide loans for others. The interest paid on these loans provides revenue for the bank, thus making the depositors' money work for them.

Tax

Setting up in business means payment of tax can be in different ways:

- Tax on individual earnings.
- Tax on profits as a sole trader or partnership.
- Corporation tax on the profits of a limited company.
- A director in a limited company pays income tax on his/her salary and also on any money withdrawn from the company.
- Value added tax.
- National insurance.

Accounts must be prepared at least once a year and even though an accountant may actually draw up the accounts, it is the owner of the business who is responsible for their accuracy and any declarations made about the profit must be correct.

If the turnover is below a set figure, which is subject to change, a summary of these accounts is all that is required.

Example

Turnover	£7103
Less Business expenses	£1299
Net profits	£5804

Turnover

This is the gross amount the business earns before deducting any business expenses. The accounts or the summary can be sent into the tax office:

- On the 5 April following the date your business started.
- The date which is twelve months after the date on which you started.
- Any date which suits your business, for example at the end of a calendar year on the 31 December or a quiet trading time when business is slow and stocks are low. For a beauty salon this could be early in the year after Christmas and New Year or in the late summer months after the busy holiday period.

The tax which has to be paid is on the profits made from the business, less allowable business expenses. In other words, any expense incurred to enable you to run your business.

Allowable expenses

These are expenses which you incur wholly in the course of running your business and may include:

- Goods and materials bought for use in the business.
- Interest on business loans.
- Hire of equipment.
- Business insurance.
- Subscriptions to professional associations.
- Advertising.
- Rent.
- Telephone.
- Heating and lighting.
- Protective clothing.
- Wages.
- Depreciation on capital items.

Depreciation

This is allowed on any capital item, for example a car or computer. A percentage of the cost is allowed to be claimed against tax each year.

Expenditure

This is the money spent in running the business and it may be classified as:

1 Capital expenditure.
2 Revenue expenditure.

Capital expenditure is used for acquiring or altering assets for use in the business, for example extending the premises, buying a motor vehicle or machinery.

Revenue expenditure is the money spent on covering the cost of everyday items such as wages, heating, replacing stock, etc.

When an expense is claimed against the business, which also has a personal use, then only the percentage which relates to the business will be allowed.

Profit and loss account

This is a summary of all the trading transactions in one year. This can be drawn up using the accounts which have been kept during the year:

○ Sales book.
○ Purchases book.
○ Petty cash book.
○ All receipts.
○ Record of wages.
○ Money drawn from the business.
○ Capital added.

Balance sheet

This is a statement of assets and liabilities of the business which may be given to the tax office with the profit and loss account.

Based on the accounts you send to the tax inspector he/she will make an assessment of how much tax is to be paid and this is usually paid in two instalments on 1 January and 1 July.

The rules on taxation are different for a sole trader and a limited company.

If you have set up a limited company you are in effect your own employer and will pay your tax through the normal PAYE system and as both employer and employee, you will have to pay both contributions.

Income tax is not paid on every penny earned; a personal allowance on which tax is not paid is given to everyone. Your accountant will advise on any other allowable business expenses.

PAYE

Once employees earn over a certain limit, tax and Class 1 national insurance, must be deducted from their wages under the Pay As You Earn (PAYE) system. The employer also pays a national insurance contribution for each employee.

Documentation
P45: Contains the employee's code number, total pay and tax deducted to date in the financial year. It must be given to the employer when the new employee starts work. The employee must provide a P45 from the previous employer which certifies the tax which has been deducted for the year so far.

P46: Obtained from the tax office by a new employee who has not paid PAYE tax before. It is a starting certificate signed by the employee and sent to the tax office, who will then give the employee an emergency code number.

P14: At the end of each tax year, all information concerning each employee's wages, income tax and national insurance contributions must be entered on a triplicate form. One copy goes to the tax office and one to the DSS.

P60: This is the third copy of the P14 which goes to the employee.

A new employee who has not paid PAYE tax before must have a P46.

To help work out the PAYE system there are two sets of tables which will be provided by the tax inspector:

1 Free pay table A.
2 PAYE taxable pay tables B–D.

Each employee has a code number and this can be found in the tables which then tells you how much tax to deduct.

Each employee has a deductions working sheet with spaces for each week of the tax year. The gross salary, tax deducted and other details are entered each time the employee is paid.

At the end of each tax year all the information concerning wages, income tax and national insurance must be entered on a form P14. One copy, the P60, is given to the employee and two copies must be sent to the tax office who will pass one copy on to the DSS.

(DSS)

National insurance

As an employer it is your responsibility to collect your employee's national insurance (NI) contributions, with their income tax and the employer's NI contribution and send them on to the Inland Revenue.

The Inland Revenue will supply you with tables to work out the contributions for all employees who are over 16 and under 60 for a

Cutting costs

Shopping around

Shop around and find a supplier of the goods you need, whose prices are lower than anyone else's. The problem that may occur is that the products may be inferior to those you are already using, or you may have to buy in such large quantities, that you are over-stocked and tying up capital, as well as risking having stock which may be out of date before you have had the opportunity to use it. If, however, the products are of an acceptable quality then this may be a successful way to increase profits.

Certain suppliers will offer a reduction on price if you deal exclusively with them. The advantages of this are:

○ Less work for the manager or stock controller in ordering goods.
○ Establishment of a good working relationship with a supplier who will advise you of new trends and special offers as your business success is also beneficial to them.

The disadvantage is that you are offering a limited range of products to your clients and providing them with less choice.

Staff cuts

Reducing staff costs by employing part-time members of staff and ensuring that the maximum number are available at the busy times and the minimum number required at the quiet times.

Opening hours

The salon's opening times could be altered to suit the clientele. For instance, if the largest percentage of clientele is the working woman it may be beneficial to have several late nights and close for several mornings when business is slow. This will save money on fixed costs which have to be paid whether business is good or bad.

Increasing the treatment range

Introducing new treatments will increase profits if there is a demand for that particular treatment. It is important, therefore, to assess the market first of all by approaching your existing clientele. If there is a positive response then offer reductions on the new treatment if a course is booked in advance. In this way revenue from advance bookings may pay for the new treatment or equipment.

The manufacturer may allow you to lease the equipment so that there is not a large capital outlay, with an option to renew the lease, or buy outright, if you decide that the treatment is successful.

By increasing the treatment range you may need to employ more staff or extend the business premises and the added costs may not be recouped very easily creating a cash flow problem, so this course of action must be seriously considered.

Increasing prices

Prices charged for treatments or products should be set initially at a level that will give you the highest profit possible. By increasing prices you run the risk of losing some clients but there are also those clients who believe that by paying a higher price for a service then it is of a higher quality and a more expensive product must be better for them and worth the extra cost. Therefore the increase in profits may more than compensate for any clients lost.

Setting a price

There is no ideal way of setting a price for services or products but there are certain considerations:

The market
The price you set is limited by the market, you have to charge what the potential client is

willing to pay. It is important, therefore, to set a price in relation to the clientele you are hoping to attract.

The product/treatment

If you have a product or new treatment which has a genuine advantage and is not provided by any other business then you can charge the highest price possible. Paying a high price also appeals to clients with high incomes or those who like to buy the most expensive products or treatments and be seen to be doing so. This is known as *price skimming*, by aiming at the cream at the top end of the market.

The competition

The services you offer and the products you sell should be looked at in relation to your competitors if their business is the same. You may be able to justify charging a higher price if your services or products are superior to those of your competitors. The areas for consideration are:

○ The quality of the service you provide.
○ The salon image.
○ The availability of products and services.
○ The reputation of your business.
○ The standard of the employees.
○ The extras you provide, for example free drinks and snacks service.

Your costs

When deciding on a price you have to take into consideration your:

○ Fixed costs.
○ Variable costs.
○ The profit you want to make.

Fixed costs are those which you have to pay whether you are actually carrying out treatments or not. So when you open up for business these are expenses which will always have to be met:

○ Rent and rates.
○ Heating and lighting.

○ Telephone.
○ Interest charges.
○ Advertising.
○ Insurance.
○ Accountancy.
○ Depreciation.
○ Wages.

Variable costs are the cost of the materials used for carrying out the treatment as these will vary with each treatment or the number of treatments carried out.

Profit is the percentage to be added to the variable and fixed costs to set your price.

Pricing strategies

Penetration pricing: Used to gain a foothold in a market with new products by pricing a product at a low level which will encourage the consumer to purchase in large quantities.

Customer value pricing: Charging the price that the consumer is prepared to pay for the product.

Price discrimination: Providing a treatment or service at different prices, this could be time based offering lower prices at quiet times to encourage sales or discounting prices for particular consumers, for example students or old age pensioners.

Market skimming: When a business has a unique product or treatment it may charge a high price for a limited period. The aim of this strategy is to make as much profit as possible while the product remains unique before the competitors join the market with something similar. When introducing new technology this strategy is often used, for example in recent years the inch loss body machines and most recently the 'non surgical facelift'.

Competition-based pricing: This strategy is used when the competition from other businesses is great and the prices charged by the competition will have a major influence on your own price.

7 Retailing

Selling more

Train your staff in sales techniques and encourage them to sell products to clients that complement the range used during their beauty treatments. While performing the treatments the therapist has the ideal opportunity to discuss with the client their beauty requirements.

Give therapists commission on their sales to encourage them to sell more. Encourage the staff to use the products they are selling so that they will sell the products from personal experience.

Take advantage of training courses provided by the manufacturers whose products you sell.

Ensure that all the staff have a good technical knowledge of all treatments and products so that they may sell with confidence.

Make sure that all the selling aids they need such as testers, free samples and product leaflets are readily available (Figure 7.1).

Record all sales on your client's record card as this will be helpful to other therapists when they are treating that client and it will allow you to contact the right people when there are special offers that they may be interested in.

Make sure the products you are selling are in stock to avoid disappointing the client.

When employing new staff, sales experience could be an important point to include in the job specification.

Place an attractive display of retail products in the salon window to catch the attention of the passer by. This could also create new business. When a prospective new client comes in to buy something on offer this will give you the opportunity to sell the beauty treatments to them.

Advertising could be worth investing more money in and also look at the type of advertising you are already using and see if it could be improved or changed.

Figure 7.1 *Retail makeup display unit*
Courtesy Depilex Limited

Provide gift vouchers for clients to give as presents as this will bring in new business as well as providing revenue.

Promote specific treatments or products at the appropriate time of the year:

○ The month leading up to Christmas is an ideal time for promoting gift sets of skin care products and makeup, when many people are looking for presents to buy.
○ In the summer months you can promote the sun protection products, false tans and treatments such as waxing, eyelash tinting, pedicures and figure correction.

o When you know that the business will be quiet, have special offers on treatments, a free gift with each booking or a reduction on the price of a treatment if the client brings along a friend at the time specified.

Retail sales

Selling retail products to clients is essential for business growth and should account for at least 40 per cent of turnover. While performing treatments there is a limit to the profit made as there are set prices for each treatment to be performed in a particular time. A specialized facial may take an hour and a half and earn £25, spend 10 minutes selling a client a set of skin care products and earn £60! The potential for increasing sales of retail products is enormous. To help there are certain considerations.

The supplier

Retail products may be obtained from:

o The manufacturer directly.
o Through a company agent or representative.
o From a wholesaler.

Wholesalers are a link between the salon and the manufacturer. They will buy products in bulk and then sell smaller quantities to retail outlets. The advantages of using a wholesaler are:

o They will offer a wide choice of products.
o They carry stock from a variety of companies.
o They provide a more personal service.
o They deliver products quickly.

Manufacturers will provide products more cheaply but may insist on larger orders which a small business may not be able to afford.

Goods may not be dispatched as quickly if the manufacturer is located in another part of the country. Sales representatives may be employed by the manufacturer to provide a more personal service which may include help with promotion of their products and advice.

Product knowledge

The management should ensure that all members of staff receive the relevant training from the manufacturers or distributors of all products sold. Being able to provide up-to-date, accurate information and explaining the features and benefits of products will inspire confidence in the client. The features describe the product and the benefits explain to the client what effects the features will achieve. Most companies provide up-to-date information through newsletters or offer a telephone helpline which salons may call for assistance.

Product display

The reception area is an ideal place for a retail display as the clients can browse when entering or leaving the salon or if they are waiting for treatment.

An eye-catching window display attracts passing trade but must be changed regularly to maintain interest and kept clean. Most companies provide display stands which show products to their best advantage. When making your own displays they must be changed regularly to maintain client interest and also to change with the season.

Each working area could have a small display of relevant products, for example skin care in a facial treatment room, aromatherapy oils in a body treatment room and sun care products in a sunbed room.

If the reception is left unattended it would be advisable to store retail products in a glass front cabinet which can be locked when unattended but the goods are on permanent display. Using a cabinet also ensures that the goods remain in good condition and do not become dusty and dirty. When products are displayed on open shelves it is a good idea to use dummy products which will be provided by some companies. This cuts down on the risk of theft as the products could be stored in a locked cupboard.

Advertising literature

Leaflets and information booklets should be available for clients to read, particularly when you are selling products which require advice in their use.

Free samples

These are not always easy to provide as not all companies have samples. When you can, provide them for the client to try particularly if the product is very expensive to buy. In this case some companies will provide 'trial size' products at a greatly reduced price for the client to buy.

Body language/ communication

Always be positive and helpful and smile when making a sale but do not stare directly at the client and intimidate her into a sale. Do not rush the sale or be too persistent in your approach as this can also be very intimidating to the client. Concentrate solely on clients, answering their questions and asking your own. Open questions should be used. These are questions which may not be answered with a yes or no; they should include words such as why, how, when, what and which, to elicit information which may help to make the sale.

Involve the clients by allowing them to smell, feel, touch and test the products.

Professional approach

Always listen to your clients and ensure that you do not miss an opportunity to sell a product to the client, in particular when they are telling you about a problem they may have, sympathize with them and then assure them that you have just the product for them. You must, however, be honest and sell clients something that will be effective.

Once you have built a good client–therapist relationship the client will always ask for your advice. You must also introduce clients to products you know will benefit them even when they have not asked. They will be relying on your expert opinion.

Link selling

When the client asks for a product always link it to another product which complements the one asked for, for example a toning lotion with a cleanser or a quick dry top coat nail polish with an enamel.

Closing the sale

This is when you feel that the time has come to complete the transaction, the client in your opinion is convinced that they want one or more of the products which are on offer.

The alternative close: This is when you will ask clients questions, such as 'Would you like the large or small size?' or 'Would you like the red or pink?' Clients will then make a decision.

The professional recommendation: This is when you are using your professional judgement in advising clients so you would say, 'I would strongly recommend that you use the primer for your brittle nails to give them flexibility and stop them from breaking.' This is the most effective as a regular client with whom you have a good relationship would not hesitate to buy what you have recommended.

The 'yes' technique: This is when you ask clients a series of questions to which they will answer 'yes', so the final question completing the sale will be answered with a 'yes'.

The elimination technique: Many clients like to feel in control of the sale so you must allow them to eliminate a number of products you are offering but make sure that you are left with an alternative.

The key to successful selling is to be honest with clients and ensure that the products you are selling to them are appropriate, will be effective in their use and good value for money.

Consumer protection

The consumer, any person who buys goods and services for money, is well protected by law and voluntary associations of traders and manufacturers, for example the Consumers Association. The greatest protection for the consumer is provided by legislation which gives them statutory rights, the most important statutes are:

The Sale of Goods Act 1979

The main points of the act are:

o The goods must be of merchantable quality so, for example, if you buy a new wax machine and discover that the heater is dented and badly scratched you would be entitled to a replacement.
o The goods must be fit for the purpose. For example, the wax machine is thermostatically controlled but the first time it is used it overheats and burns the wax when set at a low temperature. In this case you would be entitled to a full refund as the machine was not fit for the purpose.
o The goods must correspond with the description. If, for example, the model of wax machine delivered by the suppliers was not the model agreed upon, the goods were not as described and the customer is entitled to a refund.

Faulty goods should be returned immediately if one of the above conditions has been broken. If the supplier thinks the manufacturer is to blame then they must claim for them.

This act only applies to a sale between a business and the public and does not apply to sales made through classified advertisements or private transactions.

The Trade Descriptions Act 1968

This act provides protection for the consumer who has been misled or given inaccurate descriptions of goods or services offered.

The Consumer Safety Act 1978

This act lays down legal safety standards to minimize risks to the consumer from potentially harmful or dangerous products.

The Consumer Credit Act 1974

This act requires that borrowers should be made aware of the true rate of interest charged on credit facilities.

Consumer Protection Act 1987

This act implements directives laid down by the European Community providing a safeguard from products used or sold that are not safe.

The Supply of Goods and Services Act 1982

This act was introduced to improve the rights of the consumer in relation to poor service or workmanship. The act was required to make up for the short-comings of the Sale of Goods Act 1979 which applied only to the transfer of goods to the buyer from the seller and not to a situation where goods were being provided as part of a service. The conditions are the same in that goods must be of merchantable quality, fit for purpose and fit the description, but it applies to:

o Contracts for work and materials.
o Free gifts – applicable to many health and beauty establishments.
o Part exchange – a method used to update equipment.
o Contracts for hire of goods – many companies provide equipment in this way for use by the therapist.

The act also requires the person providing a service to:

○ Act with reasonable care and skill.
○ Work within a reasonable time.
○ Charge a reasonable price.

The Prices Act 1974

Prices must be displayed in such a way that it does not give a false impression.

The Resale Prices Act 1976

Manufacturers are not allowed to enforce a price at which their goods must be sold. Many companies do have a recommended retail price which they suggest a supplier should use.

The British Standards Institution

This is an independent body which establishes voluntary standards of quality and reliability. Its now famous kitemark indicates that goods conform to the high standards set by the institution. Its main objectives are:

○ The promotion of health and safety.
○ The protection of the environment.
○ The establishment of quality standards.

It provides specifications on such things as:

○ Strength.
○ Safety.
○ Quality.
○ Ingredients.

Manufacturers may submit products voluntarily for testing. If they pass they will carry a kitemark which provides the consumer with a guarantee that they are at least of reasonable quality.

Returned goods

Any business which provides retail products will, on occasion, have to deal with a customer returning goods which have been found to be unsuitable. This could be for several reasons:

○ Product is damaged.
○ Product did not work.
○ Colour not correct.
○ Product was not appropriate.
○ Out of date stock.
○ An incorrect product was originally given.

Whatever the reason, a courteous manner must be adopted as more often than not the complaint will be genuine. Even if it is not, the situation will be resolved much more quickly and effectively if the therapist adopts a professional and concerned attitude.

It is important to follow rules laid down by the management when dealing with returned goods or complaints. Listen to what the client has to say, inspect the goods, ask the client relevant questions and decide on your course of action.

When the complaint is, in your opinion, genuine, either exchange the goods or offer an alternative. When the required goods are not in stock, provide the client with a credit note, offer a refund or order a replacement which will be given to the client as soon as it becomes available.

When in doubt about the validity of the complaint, the best course of action is to refer the problem to your immediate superior, supervisor or manager.

Always keep a record of returned goods and refunds given for stock control and accounting purposes.

Contact the supplier or manufacturer of defective goods which have been returned to you and then follow their set procedure for customer complaint.

There are occasions when you may feel that the returned goods are defective through no fault of your own or your supplier. It may be in the best interest of the business to accept the returned goods and lose a small amount of money rather than lose regular income and the goodwill of a client. This is a decision which must be made by the management and is often a company policy.

Processing the sale

The receptionist will normally be responsible for taking payment from clients but each individual therapist should be familiar with all methods of payment. A procedure laid down by the management should prevent any confusion or misunderstanding.

Procedure

1 Make a record. The use of a computerized or electronic till provides an efficient method of taking money and recording sales. Numbered bills are an alternative and should include the following:
   o The name of the therapist.
   o The date.
   o All treatments.
   o All retail sales.
   o Other details, for example discount.
   o Total amount.
2 Inform the client. State clearly the total amount and show the client the itemized bill.
3 Accept payment. This may be cash, cheque, credit card, debit card or gift voucher.
4 Finalize the process. Count out the change, handing it to the client and place any notes in the till. If payment is made by any other method, follow the correct procedure.

Methods of payment

Cash
Check that notes are not forgeries by checking the water-marked picture of the Queen's head, the metallic strip running through the note, or by using an ultraviolet detector machine. Always count the change into the client's hand before placing notes into the till.

Cheque
Ensure that the cheque has been signed by the client in your presence, if not ask them to sign the back of the cheque again. Make sure that all the details are correct:

o The date.
o The correct amount in figures and numbers.
o To whom the cheque is payable.
o The signature of client.

The number of the cheque guarantee card must be written by you on the back of the cheque.

Debit card
This method of payment eliminates the need for cash or cheques. Any business that provides this service will require a special terminal through which the card will be swiped. Duplicated receipts are signed and one copy is give to the client and the other copy retained by the salon. As long as there are sufficient funds in the client's account, payment will be authorized by the bank via this computerized system.

Figure 7.2 *A example of a salon gift voucher*

Credit card

Before accepting a credit card always check the details to make sure that it is valid and has not expired. Computerized terminals may be used to swipe cards but they are not in general use in small salons which use hand-operated machines that imprint all details on a triplicate voucher.

There are several types of credit card each with their own stationery and they should be filled in using a ball-point pen. The client must be asked to check the details before signing and after ensuring the client's signature is the same as that on the card, the top copy can be given to the client. The second copy is retained by the salon and the third is sent to the credit company. The disadvantage of accepting credit cards is the charge made by the credit card company which is a percentage of the total sale.

Gift voucher

An ideal method of increasing turnover and reaching potential new clients is to offer a gift voucher scheme. Vouchers are popular particularly before Christmas or Mother's Day and can be for a particular treatment or a specific amount. When accepting a gift voucher as payment a record must be kept of the amount and serial number for accounting purposes.

8 Record keeping

The keeping of records is vital to the smooth running of a business. Therefore, it is important to develop a simple yet efficient method of organization suitable for your business.

Accounts have to be prepared for the Inland Revenue and if they are not well documented it may be difficult to work out the tax and you could end up paying more than is necessary. Accounts also have to be prepared for customs and excise if the business pays VAT and possibly the bank manager who may require information on a regular basis.

If you have formed a company then the accounts must be properly prepared for the auditor.

Detailed accounts and regular stocktaking will provide you with an immediate picture of the state of the business, allowing you to plan ahead or recognize any financial problems that may exist.

Any book-keeping system must be backed up by keeping all receipts or evidence of payments made. These should include:

o   The bank paying-in book.
o   The bank statements.
o   Check book stubs.
o   Copies of invoices, receipts and delivery notes received or given.
o   Petty cash receipts.

The books

Cash book

This will record all receipts and payments made on a daily basis. It will record what has been paid into the bank and what is taken out. At regular intervals the cash book should be added up and checked against your bank statement and this is called a bank reconciliation.

The receipts section should contain columns with the following headings:

DATE RECEIVED   INVOICE NO.   CLIENT   AMOUNT £   PAID INTO BANK

The payments column should contain columns with the following headings:

DATE PAID   CHEQUE NO.   REF   SUPPLIER   PETTY CASH   MONEY FROM BANK

There should also be a column for VAT where applicable. The more detailed the cash book is the better.

Petty cash book

This book is used to record minor transactions and would be used in conjunction with a petty cash box. A small lump sum will be drawn from the bank account, the transaction will be recorded in the cash book and placed in the petty cash box to use when necessary. When money is taken out it must be replaced with a receipt for each transaction

Each receipt should include:

o   The date of the transaction.
o   The amount of cash taken.
o   Reason for the transaction.

Sales day book

This supplies you with a record of money owed to you for goods already issued. The invoice will have been sent and a copy retained for your records which will be used to fill in details of the transaction in the sales day book. The information required would include:

o   The date.
o   The name of client.

PORTERS BEAUTY SALON
Ashley Road
Hale
Cheshire
SR5 MJ4

TEL: 0253 310717   10th April 1992

ORDER   NO: 27884

TO: ANTON COSMETICS LTD.
      5, THE GLEN
      SHREWSBURY
      JR9 AA7

CATALOGUE NO:	QUANTITY	DESCRIPTION	£	p
B20579	12	OIL OF EVENING PRIMROSE CLEANSING CREAM	24	00
B20581	12	OIL OF EVENING PRIMROSE FACE MASKS	16	00
C9362	4	EYESHADOW PALETTES	3	00
		TOTAL	43	00

SIGNED:...*Sarah Thomas*...............

Figure 8.1
Example of an order form

○ Invoice number.
○ Net amount.
○ VAT.
○ Invoice total.
○ Date it was paid.
○ Any remarks, for example not paid within the given time, etc.

Invoices should be filed away safely in numerical order and have separate files for paid and unpaid invoices.

Purchases day book

This records the money that you owe, when goods have been supplied to you and you have to pay for them within a given period. All details should be entered into the purchases book immediately and the invoice filed away with a note of the date on which the bill must be paid.

The documentation

Order forms

An order form is necessary to record your requirements so that your supplier knows exactly what you need and you have a copy for your records so that you may check your order when it arrives (Figure 8.1).

Advice notes

An advice note will be sent to you from your supplier when you have placed an order for goods. This will indicate that the order has been dealt with and the goods should arrive within the next few days. In case of a delay you will be able to inform the supplier and the problem can be dealt with.

Delivery notes

A delivery note is sent with the goods itemizing each article in the package. This will enable you to check immediately if the order is complete. If the goods cannot be examined at the time of delivery then this must be clearly marked on the copy and original that they have not been examined.

Invoices

An invoice outlines the details of the sale, the amount charged and the terms of the sale, as follows:

o   There will be an order number for you to check the goods received match the goods on the order form.
o   Terms of payment, for example cash discount for immediate payment or the length of time in which to pay.
o   Carriage, which is the cost of transporting the goods, it is sometimes paid by the supplier, if the order is above a certain amount and it would be indicated by the words 'Carriage paid'.
o   Errors or omissions in the order which will be corrected.
o   VAT.
o   The VAT registration number.
o   The invoice number, which will allow the supplier to identify the invoice immediately.

Proforma invoices
A proforma invoice is normally used when the customer's credit worthiness has not yet been established. It is an invoice which requires the customer to pay for the goods before they have been despatched.

Credit notes
A credit note will be sent by the supplier if:

o   The invoice price has to be reduced because of a mistake on the invoice.
o   Faulty goods have been returned.
o   The wrong goods were delivered.
o   An incomplete order.

These notes are often printed in red to make them easily distinguishable.

Debit notes
A debit note will be sent by the supplier if:

o   The price has to be increased because of a mistake on the invoice.
o   More goods have been sent than were ordered.

Statement of account

This is sent by the supplier on a regular basis, usually monthly, and is a record of all business transactions over that period.

Stock records

Stock control is very important to prevent running out of vital items or over purchasing. The stock should remain constant so that clients will not be disappointed when they are keen to buy something and then find that it is out of stock. Buying too much stock which remains in cupboards unsold is inefficient, as the money paid for the goods could have been used in other areas.

Efficient stock control requires:

o   One person to be responsible for stock, as the more people involved the higher the chance of mistakes being made. A stock control book or an index file for each item which must be kept up to date.
o   A minimum and maximum figure required should be included because when the stock level reaches the minimum figure the person in control will know when to re-order and maintain the correct level of goods. The maximum figure will prevent buying too much of any product and tying up business capital.

o Regular reviews of stock, which will tell you immediately the products that are selling well and those that are not.

Personnel records

These are details of the members of staff you have working for you. Records should be kept of:

o Their initial application form.
o Any relevant details from the interview.
o The contract of employment laying down their terms and conditions of employment.
o Training courses completed.
o Future plans for training.
o Personal details which could include family, absence from work, problems at work, etc. In fact, anything which may help in promoting a harmonious working relationship between employer and employee.

Wages records

These records are very important as the employer has a duty to the employee to give an itemized pay statement and to deduct tax and national insurance from their wages.

You must have:

o The name and address.
o The national insurance number.
o PAYE reference number.
o Pension details.
o Deductions which have been authorized by the employee.

Client records

These must be kept to provide certain information:

o Name, address and telephone number.
o Doctor's name, address and telephone number.
o Medical history.
o Body/skin analysis.

o Treatment record.
o Products bought.
o The name of the therapist.

These details promote confidence in your clients, of your professional abilities, reassure them that the treatment they are receiving is appropriate, even when they are being treated by a new therapist and allows a personal relationship to develop making it easier to sell the services of the salon.

It also allows for a smooth running business particularly during times of staff absences and, more importantly, provides a ready-made mailing list of clients to use when promoting new techniques or products.

The Data Protection Act 1984

Many businesses now use computers to keep records and store information about their clients. The Data Protection Act 1984 requires all personal data to be protected, therefore even if the information is just a list of names and addresses you probably need to be registered with the Data Protection Registrar. Information is available from:

Data Protection Registrar,
Wycliffe House,
Water Lane,
Wilmslow,
Cheshire
Tel: 01625 535 777
Fax: 01625 524 510

Once registered you must comply with the principles of good information handling practice, set out in the Data Protection Act:

o Obtain and process personal data fairly and lawfully.
o Hold information only for the purposes specified in your register entry.
o Use information only for those purposes and disclose it only to the people listed in your register entry.
o Only hold data which is adequate and relevant.

BEAUTY TREATMENTS

Name: ....

Address: ....

Telephone No .... Date of birth ....

How did you hear about us? ....

Are you on a diet at the moment? ....

Does any of the following apply to you : ....

Blood pressure .... Epilepsy ....

Heart disorders .... Arthritis or rheumatism ....

Diabetes .... Recent operations ....

Under medical treatment .... Taking pain killers ....

Metal implants ....

Are you or have you been pregnant in the last three months? ....

I have been familiarised with the Top to Toe treatment and I agree to use the equipment at my own risk. Furthermore, I understand that Top to Toe makes no warranties or representation regarding medical, therapeutic or cosmetic benefits either expressed or implied.

I hereby release Top to Toe, this facility and its employees from all claims now or in the future from any injury or damages in connection with the use of the equipment.

I confirm that the information provided by me is correct as of todays date and that I will inform Top to Toe immediately of any changes in circumstances relevant to the above questions.

Signature: .... Date: ....

DATE	TREATMENT	COMMENT	THERAPIST SIGNATURE

Figure 8.2 *An example of a client record card*

Stock Control System

Item	Stock Level Min.	Max.	Date Unit	Stock	Order	Stock	Order	Stock	Order	Stock	Order	Stock	Order	Stock	Order	Stock	Order	Stock	Order
1.1 Shampoo 250 ml			6																
1.3 Shampoo 250 ml			6																
1.4 Shampoo 250 ml			6																
1.5 Shampoo 250 ml			6																
1.6 Shampoo 250 ml			6																
1.1 Shampoo litre			1																
1.3 Shampoo litre			1																
1.4 Shampoo litre			1																
1.5 Shampoo litre			1																
1.6 Shampoo litre			1																
2.1 Conditioner 200 ml			6																
2.2 Conditioner 250 ml			6																
2.3 Conditioner 250 ml			6																
2.4 Conditioner 200 ml			6																
2.4s Conditioner 50 ml			6																
2.4r Conditioner 150 ml			6																
2.1 Conditioner litre			1																
2.3 Conditioner litre			1																
2.4 Conditioner litre			1																
3.4 Massage 125 ml			6																
3.5 Massage 125 ml			6																
4.0 Styling mousse 250 ml			6																
4.0 Styling gel 200 ml			6																
4.0 Styling volume 200 ml			6																
4.0 Styling volume litre			1																
5.0 Finishing control 200 ml			6																
5.0 Finishing shine 200 ml			6																
5.0 Finishing wax 75 ml			6																
5.0 Finishing control litre			1																

Figure 9.1 *A stock control form*

in their best interest to help with stock control so that you are re-ordering on a regular basis. An example of a stock control form is shown in Figure 9.1.

Storage

There should be a stock room or a large stock cupboard in which to store a larger percentage of stock. The shelving should be adjustable to allow for the difference in size of containers, particularly when buying in bulk.

Everything should be easily washable for hygiene purposes and the shelves should be clearly labelled to show exactly where each item is stored.

For safety, liquids should be stored in plastic bottles to prevent breakages and large or heavy items should be stored at the bottom or on the lower shelves.

The most frequently used stock should be placed at eye level or slightly below, to prevent unnecessary bending and stretching.

Retail products should be on display in the reception area in a glass fronted cabinet which can be locked when left unattended. There is little point having the products out of sight, as the clients will not buy them if they cannot be seen.

Shelving can be used to display retail products allowing the clients easy access but this does have several disadvantages:

1 Stock may be damaged when handled.
2 Stock can become dirty and dusty on open shelving.
3 The products could be easily stolen.

Shelving can be used to display dummy products provided by the manufacturers which will then encourage the client to ask about the products on offer.

Treatment areas should have trolleys with drawers, or small cupboards with shelves, to store a small amount of treatment products so that in the event of the therapist running out of a cream or lotion, there will be a replacement in easy reach and the therapist will not have to leave the client to go to the storeroom for the replacement.

Electrical equipment should be stored safely when not in use, covered to prevent dust accumulating and with all leads and wires securely attached.

Dangerous or hazardous chemicals should be stored in a metal cupboard away from heat and direct sunlight. Both containers and cupboard must be appropriately marked with a classification symbol devoting the hazard contained within. The classifications are:

○ Corrosive.
○ Explosive.
○ Harmful.
○ Highly inflammable.
○ Irritant.
○ Oxidizing.
○ Toxic.

The symbols are shown in Figure 4.4.

Displaying stock

Some care should be taken to display retail stock in the most eye-catching way to attract the attention of clients in the salon or potential clients who may be passing by.

Displays should always be placed in a prominent position such as:

○ The window.
○ The reception.
○ Waiting areas.
○ Treatment rooms.
○ Next to a work station.

Whatever the position of the display, it is essential that is well-maintained, clean and colourful.

The window

A salon situated at ground level provides an ideal opportunity to promote the business by using posters, products or different props and materials to promote an image. The type of display you have will depend upon the amount of window space available and if it is open with the interior of the salon clearly visible or completely closed in.

The disadvantage of a window display is that it will deteriorate when exposed to sunlight as the colours will begin to fade, liquids will evaporate and some products will change in consistency because of the increase in temperature. This problem may be overcome by using dummy products and empty boxes with posters and changing the display on a regular basis. Some of the larger companies will provide display materials and equipment as well as practical advice particularly when the business has a large account with them.

The reception/waiting areas

This is the ideal place to display retail stock as the client starts and finishes a visit here. Sometimes the client or guests will be sitting in the reception area for a period of time, providing the opportunity to browse. The attention of passers by may also be attracted by goods displayed in reception when the window is open to the salon beyond. Stock may be displayed in glass-fronted cabinets, on free-standing units or on shelves.

Treatment rooms

It is often during the course of treatment that retail sales are made and having a display of goods on offer may encourage the process.

Also being able to give the product to the clients to take out to reception when paying their bill is more likely to ensure a sale than giving them the opportunity to change their mind or forget when they have left the treatment room.

The main disadvantage is that it will make stock control slightly more difficult and clients may forget to pay if the therapist does not accompany them to reception or inform the receptionist of the purchase.

Next to a work station

Retail products for hair care may be displayed on wall-mounted units or on shelves next to the work station. Clients will be sitting facing the products while having their treatment and this provides ample opportunity for discussion and advice on home care procedures. The disadvantages are that the products are easily accessible to anyone who passes and they may become dusty and covered in hair and lacquer.

Displays should:

○ Be well balanced.
○ Use lines to draw the eye in to the focal point.
○ Reflect an image or theme.
○ Use the correct props and materials to complement the product.
○ Be colourful.
○ Achieve the desired effect.
○ Be clean.
○ Be safe and secure.

Setting up a display

Find the right location
↓
Establish objectives for the display
↓
Draw a plan
↓
Collect fixtures, props and other materials
↓
Collect items to be displayed
↓
Assemble the display safely and effectively
↓
Check the finished display conforms with the plan
↓
Check the lighting is appropriate

Figure 9.2

Stock control procedures

○ First of all choose a manufacturer or a supplier of goods who is competitively priced. To do this enquiries need to be made with several different companies until you are satisfied that you are buying the most appropriate products at a reasonable price.

It will also save a great deal of your valuable time if you find a company who deliver the goods for you and can do so in as short a time after placing the order as possible.

Discounts on large orders for prompt payment is also a plus point when choosing a supplier as this will enable you to cut your costs and increase your profits.

When purchasing stock use an official, numbered order form on which the date is written clearly, with a duplicate copy for reference in case the order arrives short or damaged. The problem is then easily dealt with if there is a copy filed away for inspection.

o Retain the advice or dispatch note the supplier will send, to inform you that the order is being dealt with. If the goods ordered do not arrive within a reasonable time the stock controller can then inform the supplier and the matter can be dealt with.

o When the goods arrive the delivery note will itemize the goods contained in the parcel, this may then be checked with the original order form and the goods in the parcel to ensure the order is complete and undamaged.

o All purchases should then be recorded in the stock book in the 'In' column.

o The new stock can then be dated and placed in the appropriate place in the stock room. New stock should be placed behind existing stock so that the products are used in strict rotation.

o Any item which is below standard or incorrect should be immediately returned to the supplier with a 'returned goods' notice, a copy of which you retain for your own records.

o If the delivery is received short of any item it is important to ring the supplier immediately if this was not noted on the delivery note and the order marked accordingly.

Computerized stock control

This is a very efficient system of stock control, particularly in the area of retail sales as the till can be linked up to a computer system, so that levels of stock are maintained and the stock required is worked out automatically.

10   *The salon and therapist*

The reception

This is a very important part of any business because the client has to enter through the reception or make an enquiry over the telephone, which is normally situated in the reception. Clients' first impressions are lasting ones, so they must be good to ensure that they feel comfortable and at ease when arriving for treatment.

The *decor* should be attractive, relaxing and inviting so that it will:

○ Make the new client feel at ease.
○ Make an existing client feel at home.
○ Encourage the prospective client passing by to want to come in to the salon and try the treatments which are on offer.

The *receptionist* should be:

○ Welcoming to all clients whether they have been attending the salon for years or if it is their first visit.
○ Helpful, as it is important that she attends to the client's needs but it is important to the therapists that she books appointments to suit them as well as accommodating the clients.
○ Patient, as she will probably have to deal with awkward clients who are not easy to please, therapists who may be overworked, and at the same time attend to all the day-to-day duties and responsibilities of the reception.
○ Pleasant and courteous as she will set the tone for the rest of the salon.

The requirements of a reception are:

○ A desk and chair for the receptionist.
○ A telephone.
○ An appointment book.
○ A till.
○ Client record cards.
○ Price lists.
○ A message pad.
○ Pen, pencil and rubber.

○ Hanging space for coats.
○ Chairs for clients.
○ Magazines.
○ Product display.
○ Product literature.
○ Plants, pictures or posters.
○ Certificates of qualification.

Duties of the receptionist

○ Answering the telephone.
○ Booking appointments.
○ Welcoming clients.
○ Dealing with problems when clients arrive late and appointments have to be re-arranged.
○ Using the till and making out bills.
○ Selling retail products.

Answering the telephone

The receptionist must have a thorough knowledge of all the treatments on offer and the prices charged so that she can answer any queries made over the telephone.

The telephone should be situated in a quiet place, which is not always possible in a busy combined hair and beauty salon.

There should be an up-to-date telephone book close by and the clients' record cards with their telephone numbers clearly marked.

The receptionist should speak clearly so that there is no misunderstanding and the caller must always be referred to by their name.

When answering the telephone the caller should be greeted in a friendly and courteous way at the same time being informed briefly of the business or person they are speaking to. For example, 'Good morning, Grange Health Hydro, Lorraine speaking, may I help you?'.

The enquiry should be dealt with in an interested and helpful way making sure that all the information the caller requires is given. If their query cannot be answered immediately then they should be asked politely to hold while another member of staff who may be able to help is sought. If this is not possible, the name and telephone number of the caller must be taken so that someone can ring back with the relevant information later in the day.

For those clients who have a habit of cancelling appointments at short notice or just not turning up, it may be worthwhile confirming their appointment by telephone the day before and the client will either cancel then, giving you the opportunity to re-book the appointment, or he/she will feel obliged to attend.

Booking appointments

An efficient system is advisable to make use of the therapist's time as this is how bookings are made for treatments. A certain length of time will be booked according to the treatment the client is having.

An appointment book with half hour blocks is necessary and it is advisable to book appointments in a regular order from the beginning of the day to the end.

If a therapist is busy all morning and a client rings for an appointment then it is more efficient to book the appointment in the first available slot after lunch rather than later in the afternoon.

Make sure that regular clients' appointments are put in the appointment book as the new pages for each month are put in. This will avoid any problems that will occur if their appointment slot is given away, particularly if they are having a course of treatments such as slimming or special facials.

Take the telephone number of a new client when booking the appointment in case you need to contact them for any reason, as there will not be a record card available.

Treatment room or area

In large businesses such as health farms and health hydros separate treatment rooms are an essential part of the business. This is because there are so many different types of treatment available. They can include:

o Swimming pool with sauna, steam and whirlpool facilities.
o A rest area.
o Multigym to cater for large numbers.
o Exercise rooms.
o Beauty rooms.
o Hair salon.

For privacy and total relaxation treatment rooms are ideal but there are many salons that do not have enough room to provide them. Therefore treatment areas should be available with curtains to provide a certain amount of privacy.

Whether the treatment room is a separate entity, a room within another salon such as hairdressing, or a room in your own home, there are certain basic items which are a necessity and others which can be added as the business grows.

Washing and drying facilities are a must so ensure that there are plenty of clean towels available. The need for clean towels can be reduced considerably by the use of disposable paper towelling to protect the bedding.

Facial work

o A multipurpose treatment couch which allows different treatments to be performed.
o A sink unit with storage space underneath for towels, treatment products and tools.
o A trolley to hold equipment, cosmetics, treatment materials and with a small drawer to store small implements.
o A magnifying mirror for close inspection of the skin.
o A sterilizing unit.
o Depilatory waxing unit for legs, arms and face.
o A selection of facial equipment which may be chosen according to the client's requirements, the working capital you have available and your specialist skills. They may include:
–Facial steamer.
–High frequency.
–Vacuum suction.

environment and prevents them from having to stand around in the salon when they are not busy.

Image

Selecting the image for any business is very important as it provides an instant visual picture to prospective clients. Image may be expressed in terms of:

o The location of the business.
o The external appearance of the salon.
o The name and logo.
o The interior decor.
o The staff uniforms or clothes.
o The prices charged.
o The products used and treatments offered.
o The ambience or atmosphere created.
o The stationery, price lists, gift vouchers and business cards.

Hairdressing salons give much thought to image when designing a new salon or re-designing an existing salon, to make it stand out from its competitors. The image varies depending on the market it is aiming for, the type of clientele it already has, fashion or even a reflection of the owner's personality or taste. Some recent examples include:

o The minimalist approach with a neutral colour scheme.
o A fantasy theme with unusual colours and design.
o High tech and ultra modern.
o A step back in time with Victorian furniture and old-world charm.
o Glamorous, luxury.

The music played in a salon may also reflect the image and a hairdressing salon has a larger choice because of the nature of the service.

Holistic therapists such as reflexologists and aromatherapists create an image of quiet calm and reassurance because the services they offer are an antidote to the stresses and strains of modern life. The location for their service is quite often part of another complementary business again reflecting their own image, this may be:

o A beauty salon.
o A medical centre.
o A centre for holistic therapies.
o Health and holistic establishments.
o Private practice.

Beauty salons also portray different images depending on the location of the business, the market they are aiming for or the treatments they specialize in, the variation may include:

o A salon within a health and fitness club providing services for members and the general public. The types of treatment offered will probably be mostly body treatments, weight reduction programmes, exercise classes and holistic therapies.
o A beauty room within a hairdressing salon providing treatments such as manicure, pedicure, waxing, makeup and other basic beauty treatments.
o A beauty salon which provides a full range of treatments but uses and sells products from one large company which provides the salon image because of the famous name and logo.
o A beauty salon which creates its own image by specializing in particular treatments or concepts, for example natural beauty, weight reduction, specialized treatments such as electrolysis, thread vein removal or false nails.
o A spa offering hydrotherapy, beauty and holistic therapies.

Salon security

It is in the best interests of a salon owner to ensure that the property and contents of the business are well-insured to cover all risks. There will be certain steps to follow to reduce the risks of burglary or theft from the premises from any person who may enter as a client, member of staff or business contact.

Premises
o Install a burglar alarm which will help to deter burglars – some sophisticated alarms are linked directly with the police or to a security firm who have the facility to detect movement and sound inside the premises.

○ If the salon has a large window frontage make sure it is made from toughened glass and contains an alarm in the form of a metal strip across the full length of the window.

○ Check that the locks on all the doors and windows are up to standard and if not ask for advice from the insurance company about the correct type of lock that should be fitted.

○ Key holders should be appointed to open and lock the salon daily. These people should also be known to the police in case the premises are broken into outside opening hours.

○ Provide some sort of night lighting to provide a clear view into the salon as a deterrent and to help security.

Money

○ Use an electric till, one which can be locked or a cash box kept in a drawer or cupboard which may be locked.

○ If possible appoint one person to be responsible for the handling of cash.

○ Pay money taken daily into the bank before they close.

○ Store money taken after banking hours in a safe. This may also be used for any valuables inadvertently left on the premises.

○ Leave the till drawer open at night to show that it is empty.

Stock

○ Appoint one person to be responsible for stock control.

○ Therapists should sign for stock when it is required for treatments.

○ Store consumable products in a locked store room or cupboard.

○ Check stock regularly.

○ Retail products should be displayed in a locked glass fronted cabinet.

○ Use only dummy products on open display.

○ Keep records up to date.

Clients' property

○ Place jewellery and valuables in a safe place in the treatment room. If the room is left unattended ensure that the valuables are locked away or out of sight.

Staff property

○ Provide lockers or lockable cupboard in the staff room for staff members to store their property.

The therapist and hairdresser

It is extremely important to present a professional, courteous and warm image to your clients, to instil confidence, provide reassurance and make them all feel welcome. This initial contact will determine whether the client becomes a loyal and regular client or takes the business elsewhere. The management will set standards of appearance, hygiene and conduct and it is the duty of the employee to maintain these standards.

Client consultation

Apart from providing an efficient and effective service to satisfy the requirements of your clientele, the most important procedure for any therapist or hairdresser is the consultation with a client which occurs naturally during each appointment and in particular, the initial consultation.

Communication must be effective as the outcome of this contact should be a satisfied client with whom you have established a long-term professional relationship for your mutual benefit. Clients will receive the service that they require and you will be increasing the profits.

Sufficient time must be allocated for the initial consultation as it is important to make the client feel relaxed, comfortable and assured of your individual attention. Detailed records will be taken and they must be accurate and concise to provide relevant information for all those concerned with treating the client.

The location for consultation must be private to reassure the client that any personal information that they provide for the therapist is given in the strictest confidence. When clients are attending for body treatment they may need to be measured therefore privacy is an essential. Clients may also feel nervous and reluctant to speak openly when there are other people in close proximity.

With a new client attending for epilation it is necessary to make detailed records which will enable the therapist to plan the appropriate treatment. Medical history is important and a short treatment may be given at the consultation therefore a private treatment room is the most appropriate place.

Consultation in a hairdressing salon is far more relaxed and informal. The client often requires advice before changing hair colour or style and relevant information such as name, address and telephone number needs to be recorded at the initial consultation with details of products used for future reference. The location will probably be in the salon itself as it may be necessary to test the hair before recommending treatment, or the skin to ensure compatibility with products to be used.

Consultation is necessary:

○ To provide information to your client about treatments, services and products.
○ To record information about the client to ensure the correct treatment is provided.
○ To recognize contraindications and identify conditions which may require treatment to be adapted or to receive special treatment or advice.
○ To recognize any factor which may limit or affect the services offered.
○ To allow the client to seek clarification regarding the treatment, products, appointment times and cost.
○ To mutually agree on results to be achieved.
○ To promote a professional relationship with your client.
○ To gain the trust of your client.

Qualities

The therapist should be:

Friendly: To make people feel welcome.
Sincere: Putting the best interests of the client first.
Honest: Never mislead or provide the client with unrealistic expectations.
Cheerful: To relax the client and promote a pleasant atmosphere.
Polite: Treat all clients with equal respect no matter how difficult they may be.
Discreet: The client must feel secure in the knowledge that any personal information or anything which has been said in confidence will not be passed on.

Approachable: Allows clients to communicate their requirements.

Appearance

The therapist should:

○ Wear a clean, loose-fitting and well-pressed uniform.
○ Wear comfortable low-heeled shoes.
○ Wear the minimum amount of jewellery – small stud earrings and a wedding ring is acceptable.
○ Wear well-applied and discreet makeup which will look good even in warm working conditions.
○ Make sure hair is clean and well-groomed. If it is below chin length it should be tied back so that it does not fall in the eyes or over the client.
○ Have well-manicured, short nails which allow treatments to be performed effectively and hygienically.
○ Practise good hygiene:
  –Bathe daily.
  –Use an antiperspirant.
  –Wash hair regularly.
  –Change underwear daily.
  –Clean teeth morning and night and after eating.
  –Use breathfreshener.

Hairdressers are more flexible in approach to their appearance:

○ Clothing must be comfortable and allow ease of movement although the style will reflect the image a salon wishes to portray.
○ Protective clothing such as aprons and gloves will be worn for applying tints, perms and bleaches.
○ It is advisable to wear fabrics which do not attract hair such as polycotton which allows the hair to slide off easily.
○ Comfortable shoes are important as the hairdresser is standing for many hours during the day. They should be closed to prevent loose hairs from penetrating the skin.
○ The hairstyle is an important aspect of a hairdresser's appearance as it will reflect the image and ability of the salon, it should therefore always be clean, well-cut and styled.

Behaviour

The therapist must act in a professional manner towards clients, colleagues, suppliers and competitors:

- When treating clients, always give them your undivided attention and ensure that treatment is appropriate.
- Do not discuss your personal problems and avoid controversial topics of conservation.
- Always co-operate with your colleagues and become a reliable and effective member of the team.
- Always be hard-working and conscientious using initiative in all aspects of work.
- Always be open and honest in communications with management and show a willingness to learn and improve on skills and experience.
- Always be ethical in your behaviour by respecting other therapists and following the code of conduct laid down by the professional association to which you are affiliated.

Client care

Once a professional relationship has been established the therapist or hairdresser must provide a high standard in client care to retain their loyalty.

It will be the responsibility of the management to ensure that all members of staff are providing the same standards, through training and appraisal.

Good client care requires the management to:

- Employ competent staff to provide effective treatment.
- Ensure the salon is open at times to accommodate all clients.
- Offer an 'at home' service when required, for example weddings, at times outside normal working hours or when the client is unable to attend the salon for treatment due to illness or injury.
- Ensure that all members of staff keep up-to-date with new treatments, innovations and products.
- Provide facilities for the disabled client.
- Keep clients informed of all special offers and promotions.

- Listen courteously to any complaints or grievances and resolve problems quickly and equitably.
- When the client enters the salon:
  - Greet warmly.
  - Take their outdoor garments and provide any necessary gowns or robes.
  - Keep to appointment times.
  - If the client is unavoidably kept waiting offer a drink and an up-to-date magazine to read.
  - Give your client your undivided attention during treatment.
  - Do not leave the client alone unnecessarily.
  - Accommodate all reasonable requests.
  - Escort the client to reception after treatment.
  - Organize the client's next appointment.

Code of ethics

Many professional associations and organizations will have their own code of ethics which is a set of guidelines that impose various obligations on their members, to ensure that members of the public are protected from improper practice.

The code will be implemented by the organization by issuing a set of rules and regulations which establish the required conduct expected of its members.

The code will:

- Establish appropriate conduct.
- Establish acceptable practices.
- Protect clients or consumers from improper practices.
- Maintain professional standards of behaviour towards
  - Other members of the organization.
  - Members of the public and clients.
  - Other professional therapists.
  - Members of other professional organizations.
  - Colleagues within the industry.

In general all professional therapists and hairdressers should:

- Comply with statute law and local bylaws.
- Apply treatments for which they are qualified.
- Not treat a client who may be contraindicated.

o Consult with the client's medical practitioner when necessary.
o Maintain client confidentiality.
o Treat colleagues with respect.
o Not criticize other businesses.
o Not deliberately poach clients from a competing business.

Professional associations

Association of Reflexologists
27 Old Gloucester Street
London
WC1N 3XX

British Association of Beauty Therapy and Cosmetology
Parabola House
Parabola Road
Cheltenham
Gloucestershire
GL50 3AH

British Association of Electrolysists
18 Stokes End
Haddenham
Buckinghamshire
HP17 8DX

British Association of Skin Camouflage
25 Blackhorse Drive
Silkstone Common
Near Barnsley
South Yorkshire
S75 4SD

The Federation of Holistic Therapists
38A Portsmouth Road
Woolston
Southampton
SO19 9AD

The Guild of Professional Beauty Therapists Ltd
Guild House
PO Box 310
Derby
DE23 9BR

Independent Professional Therapist International
8 Ordsall Road
Retford
Nottinghamshire
DN22 7PL

International Aestheticians
Bache Hall
Bache Hall Estate
Chester
CH2 2BR

International Federation of Aromatherapists
Department of Continuing Education
Royal Masonic Hospital
Ravenscourt Park
London
W6 OTN

International Society of Professional Aromatherapists
Hinckley and District Hospital and Health Centre
The Annexe
Mount Road
Hinckley
Leicestershire
LE10 1AE

11 *Starting your own business*

Running a business is not easy. It provides job satisfaction and independence but means longer working hours, fewer holidays and, to begin with, lower earnings. Commitment is essential and those who produce a good business plan are more likely to succeed. The initial steps to success include the following:

Finding the right location for a new business

There must be a demand for the services in the area for your business to be successful.

If there are already established businesses in the chosen location find out about the type of treatments on offer and check out their strengths and weaknesses. There is little point setting up an identical business in opposition to an already thriving one. It may be better to research other locations until a more suitable one is found.

Buying an existing business

It is important to find out exactly why a business is up for sale. There are many reasons why businesses are sold but the owner of the business you are interested in may feel that it is under threat or not a viable business and is cutting his/her losses and running. When you are completely satisfied that everything is above board then it is time to examine all aspects of the business.

A thriving beauty business is reliant on the continuing patronage of the existing clientele. Therefore, it is important to obtain an undertaking from the present owner that he/she will not be opening up elsewhere in competition with you and the clients will be remaining with the salon.

The sale price may include equipment which will only be of use to you if it is in good working order and has a long working life ahead of it. It would be worthwhile, therefore, to have everything checked by an expert.

Retail stock must be up-to-date and preferably of products which will be easy to sell.

Have the accounts for the last few years checked by an accountant to ensure the business is profitable.

A business from home

The idea of working from home is very appealing as there would be no travelling to and from work and the hours worked could fit in with your normal daily routine.

Such a business is only viable if there is the room available to use for the salon. Space such as a loft or an integral garage could be converted but first it is necessary to determine what equipment and furniture will be required and this will indicate how much space will be needed.

Since many beauty therapy equipment manufacturers now make combined self-standing units, it is possible to offer a variety of different face and body treatments in a limited space.

Before making any decisions it is important to ascertain if you are legally entitled to use your home for business. Planning permission must be sought if the business will materially change the use of your home. This is open to interpretation by different local authorities.

Check the deeds of the house to ensure there are no clauses to prevent part of the house being used for business purposes. In the case of your home being mortgaged it is important to check the documents to ensure there is no breach of contract.

The insurance cover may need to be changed on your home when using it for business so check with your insurance company for advice.

Mobile beauty business

A mobile business is an increasingly popular option for the many fully trained beauty therapists who want to specialize in one particular treatment. There are also many more individuals who are training in just one specialized subject. These specialisms include:

- Aromatherapy.
- Reflexology.
- Body massage.
- Sports therapy.
- Electrolysis.
- Makeup artist.
- Nail technician.
- Hairdresser.

Advantages

- There is a captive market as there are many prospective clients who cannot leave home because they are disabled or elderly, are a carer looking after a relative, are without transport, or even agoraphobic. In rural areas there may not be a beauty salon and travelling to the nearest large town or city may be time-consuming, inconvenient and expensive.
- There is a relatively small capital outlay particularly when specializing in one particular treatment as the mode of transport is the largest expense.
- Overheads are low as the location for business is the client's own premises which could be a home or workplace.
- It is easier to offer a specialized service, for example aromatherapy.
- A choice of working hours and flexibility is available to the mobile therapist allowing other commitments to be accommodated without having to consult with colleagues or superiors.
- The service is more personal and a good client therapist relationship is easily established and maintained.

- There are increased benefits to clients because they will not have to travel and treatments will be far more relaxing.

Disadvantages

- A limited number of treatments may be achieved in a day because of the time needed to travel. Planning of appointments will be essential to prevent unnecessary time being wasted.
- It is necessary to carry all equipment and products required to ensure an efficient service so good planning and organization are essential
- Equipment may get damaged.
- Setting up equipment may be difficult depending on the location to be used for the treatment.
- Business expansion is difficult.
- There are risks involved when attending new clients. It is important, therefore, to vet any prospective clients or rely on personal recommendation.

Considerations

- The local authority bylaws should be checked before offering a mobile service to ensure that all regulations are complied with.
- Registration will be required for electrolysis and ear piercing.
- Many suppliers of equipment will supply special mobile units in a protective carrying case which will reduce the risk of damage occurring in transit.
- Some product suppliers also provide cushioned carrying cases to prevent accidents.
- Lightweight sturdy equipment is a must for mobile businesses to prevent therapists suffering from back strain or injury when loading or unloading.
- Team up with a mobile hairdresser and share client lists. It will help to increase business and ensure clients are recommended.

Franchising

Franchise: Is a licence to operate a business in a particular area, given by a business with an established name and reputation.
Franchisee: This is the person who buys the franchise.
Franchiser: This is the person who sells the franchise.

The basic principle involved in franchising is when a successful company that manufactures, retails products or provides a service decides to expand its business by becoming a franchiser instead of opening up other branches which are owned by its parent company.

The company is selling its already established reputation and valuable expertise to a franchisee. In effect, the franchisee is buying a complete business system or way of trading.

The franchisee enters into a contract to sell the product or provide the service under the franchiser's name, following strict guidelines laid down by the franchiser.

The legal form the franchise will take will be the same as any other business, that is, sole trader, partnership or limited company.

Advantages

The chief advantage of starting a business by buying a franchise is that all the problems normally encountered when running a business from scratch will already have been analysed and solved and, with a reputable franchiser, there is a greater chance of success:

○ The business is your own.
○ There are reduced risks in the setting up of the business as the problems have been solved by the franchiser.
○ There is continuing support provided by the franchiser which is particularly good for those inexperienced in business.
○ The product or service bought has a recognizable name with an established reputation.
○ The business will benefit from the advertising and promotion carried out by the franchiser.
○ Previous experience is not necessary in most cases, for example retail sales, as training is normally given by the franchiser.

Disadvantages

○ There will be restrictions on how the business is run as all business transactions must be in the best interest of the franchiser and the other franchisees.
○ There is usually a large initial fee to be paid for the franchise.
○ Subsequent payments must then be paid each year usually as a percentage of turnover.
○ The franchiser has the right to come to the business premises to inspect records, and sales statistics have to be sent on a regular basis.
○ Operating methods laid down by the franchiser have to be strictly adhered to which may prevent franchisees using their own initiative and expertise.
○ All stock may have to be purchased from the franchiser, not allowing the franchisee freedom to seek competitive alternatives.
○ If the franchisee wants to sell the business before the end of the contract the franchiser has to agree.
○ The franchise runs for a set number of years with an option to renew 'if the franchisee's performance is satisfactory'. This may mean a commitment to spending more on refurbishment.
○ If the franchisee cannot renew there may be little to sell as the franchisee cannot sell the name and goodwill.

Precautions

○ An accountant should examine the forecasts given by the franchiser.
○ A solicitor should go through any contract before it is signed to see how the franchiser is making money and to analyse the restrictions they may impose.
○ The franchisee should find out how many franchises have already been sold and how long they have been trading.

○ The franchisee should talk to existing franchisees.

Expert advice

It is most important to consult experts who have the knowledge to help you turn an idea into a thriving business and by consulting the right people you will ensure the advice you are given is both relevant and professional.

Enterprise agencies

Many local authorities, supported by private industry, central and local government, provide training courses in starting and running your own business. The aim of these agencies is to promote economic growth and employment opportunities in local communities. Specialists from the area in which you hope to work are available to offer expert advice and they come from:

○ Supporting businesses.
○ The professions such as solicitors and accountants.
○ Financial institutions.
○ Local authorities.
○ Government departments.

The help they provide includes the following:

○ How to start up your business.
○ Financial and legal considerations.
○ Marketing.
○ Finding premises.
○ Business planning.
○ Obtaining grants.
○ Accounts, budgets and cash flow.
○ Developing an existing business.

There are courses run by the Manpower Services Commission which vary from one week to sixteen and details of these can be obtained from your local job centre.

There are various government agencies whose existence is specifically for providing assistance to new business ventures. These agencies provide schemes which give free business advice, counselling and training. The schemes may provide an allowance for a short time which provides financial assistance through the difficult start-up period. Certain conditions have to be met to receive the allowance and these relate to:

○ Benefits received.
○ Your employment situation.
○ Your age.
○ The hours you have to work in the business.
○ Your own financial commitment.
○ The business must also be approved by the Department of Employment.

As specific conditions and requirements are subject to change, current up-to-date information may be obtained from:

The Manpower Services Commission,
Moorfoot,
Sheffield S1 4PQ.
Telephone number: 0114 275 3275.

Banks

Most of the major banks have a business adviser who will offer advice to anybody starting their own business and can help in planning sensibly for the future. The bank is there not only to lend money but also to create successful businesses. Therefore, they are pleased to help even if they do not provide the capital.

The bank manager may decide to lend you money for your business after you have presented him/her with a viable business plan and the bank will advise you of the full range of services available and provide support and advice to prevent problems occurring.

Accountants

An accountant can be of great help to you. In presenting your case to your bank manager, when you are trying to raise capital for your business, an accountant will have the experience to present your case in the most acceptable form, increasing your chances of approval.

Once the business is assured the accountant can help set up an efficient accounting system which will allow you to find out quickly and easily how your business is doing.

Accountants can also prepare salary structures and provide advice on the company formation and the legal structure of the business.

They will explain the tax laws and advise you on how to obtain the maximum tax relief (the reduction you can make in your tax bill by deducting legitimate expenses, which can be many and varied, from the overall tax liability).

It is important to ensure that your accountant is properly qualified, so choose an accountant in your area from:

The Institute of Chartered Accountants,
PO Box 433,
Chartered Accountants Hall,
Moorgate Place,
London EC2P 2BJ.

The Chartered Association of Certified Accountants,
29 Lincoln's Inn Fields,
London WC2.

Solicitors

Choose a solicitor who specializes in commercial law and provide him/her with copies of all relevant documentation including your business plan.

A solicitor will help in various ways:

o   Advising you on any business contracts.
o   Helping you to understand employment laws and draw up contracts of employment.
o   Negotiating leases and conveyancing on business premises.
o   Drafting company rules and partnership agreements.

Solicitors' fees are quite high, so if you need free legal advice contact the Citizens Advice Bureau who will provide you with all the necessary details.

Insurance broker

The best way to ensure you have adequate insurance cover is through a broker. To obtain a list of insurance brokers in your area contact:

The British Insurers Association,
Fountain House,
14 Bevis Marks,
London EC3A 7NT.

Telephone number: 0171 623 9043

12 Finding the right location and premises

For your business to be successful you must have the right premises, in the right area and at the right price. This may prove to be quite difficult but it is important not to compromise and accept premises which you consider to be second best.

Because you are providing a service the business should:

○ Be centrally situated in a well-populated area.
○ Provide the services the area requires, a fact which should already have been gleaned from your market research.
○ Provide services which either differ from, or are better than your competitors.
○ Be close to other businesses which have a brisk trade, for example a bank or post office, as there will be people constantly passing.
○ Be near to other businesses which may complement your own and bring in new clients, for example a hairdressers or a chemist.
○ Be easily accessible to drivers and those using public transport.

There is a current trend for beauty therapists to share premises with aromatherapists, reflexologists and other alternative therapists as well as chiropodists, the main advantages being the sharing of costs and the gaining of clients from the other practices.

The premises

The options when you have found the ideal premises are to lease or to buy.

Leasing

Leasing has the advantage that any existing capital will be available for use within the business rather than being tied up in buying a property, with mortgage repayments that could be a burden.

When negotiating the lease it may be advisable to go for as short a lease as possible with the option to renew the lease for a longer period when you feel sure that the business is going to be a success.

It is important, however, to allow your solicitor to advise you as he/she is the expert in these matters.

The disadvantages are that over a long period of time the lease will cost as much if not more than buying the premises.

Although you have the right to agree new terms for the lease when the present one expires, landlords can refuse if you have not been a good tenant or if they require the premises for their own occupation then they may be able to take possession but they will have to pay you compensation.

You must seek the landlord's permission for any alterations you may wish to make.

Before signing a lease it is important to check the following:

○ That the premises can be used for a beauty salon or the purpose you require.
○ Who is responsible for the repair and maintenance of the premises.
○ What is the length of the lease (the length can vary considerably).
○ Is subletting part or all of the premises permitted.
○ How often is the rent reviewed.

o Are there any major works planned to improve the area which may affect your business?

The Landlord and Tenant Act 1954

The purpose of this act is to give the tenant some security in remaining in the premises after the lease has expired and to be compensated for improvements which add to the value of business premises.

The landlord has to give six months' notice if the lease is to be terminated. This will give the tenant the opportunity to apply to the court to have the lease renewed. The court may refuse the application if the landlord can show the following:

o The rent is in arrears.
o The property has been allowed to fall into disrepair.
o The landlord has found alternative premises for the tenant.
o The premises are to be demolished or reconstructed.
o The landlord needs the premises for his/her own occupation.

If the court orders termination of the lease and the tenant is not at fault then the tenant has the right to compensation from the landlord.

The tenant has the right to compensation for improvements to a lease if the work was undertaken:

o After the landlord has been given notice of the tenant's intention to make the improvements.
o The improvements were undertaken with the approval of the landlord.

Buying

Buying has the advantage of being a sound investment, if a good property is bought at the right price and then sold at a profit after some years.

The disadvantages are that it may be difficult to obtain a commercial mortgage for a new business so the problem lies in raising the money to purchase the property.

The money you have available to invest may be more profitably invested in the business rather than the property itself.

The salon

The image a beauty salon presents is very important especially with competition close by. Therefore, the appearance must be attractive to the type of client you hope to draw. The correct image must be achieved at a reasonable cost which still allows you to work profitably.

The salon should provide adequate space for the staff you hope to employ, to work comfortably and efficiently. Look for premises which have the following services and facilities installed:

o Telephone system.
o Burglar alarm.
o Heating.
o Adequate lighting.
o Electricity points.
o Air conditioning and ventilation.

The name

Choosing a name is not something to rush into because once it has been chosen and placed in a prominent position above the business it will probably remain, and a mistake could adversely affect the business.

Creating the right image is important and the image of the salon will be reflected in the name. It should also identify the services you are selling to the client and convey a message to both new and existing clients.

Try the name out on people first, asking them to describe the picture it conjures up in the mind.

Make sure the name you have chosen is original. If the business is to be entered in *Yellow Pages* then it may be advisable to choose a name which begins with a letter from the beginning of the alphabet so the client will ring your number first.

The choice of name must conform to the rules laid down by The Companies Act 1985 and The Business Names Act 1985. The main purpose of these acts is to enable anyone dealing with a business to know the owner's name and address.

According to the act the owner of the business must disclose his/her surname ás a sole trader, all surnames in a partnership and the full corporate name if it is a limited company and in each case the address. This information must appear on all stationery if trading under a name other than the surname or corporate name.

13 Business status

One of the most important decisions to make when opening a business is the legal form the business will take. There are three options:

1 Sole trader.
2 Partnership.
3 Limited company.

Each one of these options has its advantages and disadvantages.

Sole trader

To start up as a sole trader all you have to do is inform your local tax inspector and DSS office with little effort and few formalities. Being a sole trader means that you are solely responsible for the business and liable for all the money the business owes. When there is not enough money in the business, all personal possessions, including your home, could be taken to settle debts. All the profits, however, belong solely to you.

Accounts do not have to be submitted to Companies House but annual accounts do have to be submitted to HM Inspector of Taxes.

As a sole trader income tax is paid at the normal rate and is paid on a preceding year basis. This means that tax may be paid on profits up to two years afterwards and this helps a small business with cash flow.

Self assessment begins for tax returns issued from April 1997. The rules applying to self-employed people are published in a booklet entitled *Self Assessment – A guide for the self-employed*, a copy of which can be obtained from your tax office.

You are not answerable to anyone else for decisions you make regarding the business.

When using a trade name you must put your name and address as proprietor on all business stationery and on a notice displayed on the business premises.

Partnership

This is where there are a minimum of two people or a maximum of twenty people who will provide the start-up cash and share the workload in a business.

In a business partnership there may be either a full partner who will participate fully and share both the profits and losses or a sleeping partner who takes no active part in the running of the business but who provides working capital and does take responsibility for any debts but only up to the amount they have put in the business.

As each partner is responsible for the debts of the others it is advisable for a partnership agreement to be drawn up by a solicitor so that each partner has some sort of protection.

The partners should agree on certain things:

○ The name of the business.
○ The date the partnership will start and how long it will last.
○ The amount of capital to be provided by each partner.
○ Who is authorized to operate bank accounts.
○ How the business will be managed and what each partner's responsibilities will be.
○ How the profits will be divided.
○ What provision will be made for holidays and other time off.
○ What will happen in the event of a partner withdrawing from the partnership for whatever reason, for example retirement or leaving.
○ What provision will be made in the event of the death of a partner.
○ Arrangements for admitting new partners.
○ The conditions under which the partnership may be terminated in case of a dispute.
○ The arrangements to be made for the dissolving of the partnership.

If there is no agreement then any of the partners can pull out of the partnership at any time, leaving the other partners to find the money to buy out their share of the business.

Limited company

Forming a limited company is more complicated than a partnership and advice must be sought from a solicitor. When a limited company is set up a new legal entity is being created. A company must have at least two shareholders, one director and a company secretary who may also be a director.

The company must be registered with the Registrar of Companies and the following should be provided:

○ Memorandum of association.
○ Articles of association.
○ Various forms.
○ A registration fee.

The Certificate of Incorporation should be on public display. There is also certain information which must be displayed on all stationery and letterheads:

○ The registered name and address in full.
○ The place of registration.
○ The registration number.
○ Either all or none of the directors' names.

The advantages of a limited company

The main advantage of a limited company is that the shareholders have a limited liability for debts. They are not personally responsible for the company's debts and creditors may only claim on the assets of the company and not on personal assets.

Other advantages are that a limited company may lend credibility to your business and investors and creditors may have greater confidence.

There is a lower tax rate payable on profits under £200,000.

The disadvantages of a limited company

It can cost up to £200 to register if you use an agent.

Annual accounts have to be submitted to Companies House.

The details of the company are open to public scrutiny.

An annual meeting of members is compulsory.

The directors are subject to company law and have responsibilities to act in the best interests of the company and its shareholders, answering personally for failure to do so.

Naming the business

A sole trader is not obliged to register the name of the business if it is not their own name, but it must not be too much like a name already in existence, as this may be construed as misleading the public.

Their own name, however, must figure prominently on:

○ Business letters.
○ Written orders for goods.
○ Invoices.
○ Written demands for payment of debts.

When a limited company is formed the name must be registered with Companies House and it must not be identical to any other company's name.

The name must not be considered illegal or offensive and it must not contain the word 'limited' anywhere in the name but at the end.

There are two leaflets produced by the Department of Trade and Industry and may be obtained from:

Companies House,
Crown Way,
Cardiff CF4 3UZ.

They are entitled *Disclosure of Business Ownership* and *Control of Business Names*.

14　The business plan

An essential ingredient in a successful business is to have *a business plan*, a document which details the business you hope to start and the expectations you have for its success for at least the first year (Figure 14.1).

This is helpful to yourself in establishing your business as it is valuable for reference when so many day-to-day problems are diverting your attention from your long-term business objectives.

The business plan lays down these objectives allowing you to follow your plan closely and keep it on course. The plan is also helpful in presenting your case when applying for a loan.

The plan should be divided into two parts:

1 A section about the business itself which will allow the reader to assess instantly whether this business venture has the potential for success.
2 A financial section to present your case to the bank or possible investors in such a way that you will secure the capital you require to start up.

INTRODUCTION

DETAILS OF THE BUSINESS
Name of business
Business address

Business status
Type of business
Telephone
Date business began (if youhave already started trading
Business activities

PERSONAL DETAILS
Name
Address

Telephone (home)   Telephone (work)
Qualifications

                                                          Date of birth
Relevant work experience

Business experience

Course attended

Details of key management personnel (if any)

Name	Name
Position	Position
Address	Address
Date of birth	Date of birth
Qualifications	Qualifications
Relevant work experience	Relevant work experience
Present income	Present income

What skills will you need to buy in during the first two years?

PERSONNEL
Estimate the cost of employing any people or buying any services you may need in the first two years

Number of people	Job function	Monthly cost	Annual cost

(Remember to include your own salary and those of any partners you may have in this calculation)
PRODUCT/SERVICE
Description

continued

Figure 14.1 *The business plan*

Contribution of individual products or services to total turnover

Product	% Contribution
	(the figures in this column should add up to 100)

Break down the cost of materials (if any)

PRODUCT A

Materials (including packaging, labelling etc.)	Cost

*Selling price for Product A:

PRODUCT B

*Selling price for Product B:

PRODUCT C

*Selling price for Product C:

(*These are assumptions)

Where did you get your estimate from?

Material	Source

MARKET

Describe your market

Where is your market?

Who are your customers?

Is your market growing, static or in decline?

Itemise the competitive products or services

Competitor's name

Competitors product/service A

Name	Price
Strengths	Weakness

Competitor's name

Competitors product/service B

Name	Price
Strengths	Weakness

Competitor's name

Competitors product/service C

Name	Price
Strengths	Weakness

What is special about your own product or service?

Advantages of your product or service over

Competitor A

continued

Competitor B

Competitor C

What is your sales forecast for the
*1st three months?
Treatments/products   Total value
*2nd three months?
Treatments/products   Total value
*3rd three months?
Treatments/products   Total value
*4th three months?
Treatments/products   Total value
(*These are assumptions)

Explain how you have arrived at these estimates

Give details of any firm orders you already have

MARKETING
What sort of marketing do your competitors do?
Competitor A

Competitor B

Competitor C

What sort of marketing or advertising do you intend to do?
Method   Cost

Why do you think that these methods are appropriate for your particular market?

Where did you get your estimates from?
Method   Source

PREMISES/EQUIPMENT/PRODUCT
PREMISES:
Where do you intend to locate the business and why?

What sort and size of premises will you need?

What are the details of any lease, licence, rent, rates and when is the next rent review due?

What equipment & products do you require?

Is equipment bought or leased and how long is their life span?

On what terms will the products be purchased?

continued

The business plan – continued

RECORD SYSTEM
Describe records to be kept and how they are to be kept up to to date?

OBJECTIVES
What are your personal objectives in running the business?
Short-term

Medium-term

How do you intend to achieve them?

What objectives do you have for the business itself?
Short-term

Medium-term

How do you intend to achieve them?

What are your long-term objectives (if any)
1.

2.

3.

4.

5.

How do you intend to achieve them?

FINANCE
Give details of your known orders and sales (if any)

Date	Orders/sales	Details	Delivery date
1			
2			
3			
4			

Give details of your current business assets (if any)

Item	Value	Life expectancy

What will you need to buy to start up and then throughout your first year?
Start up

Item	Value

Year 1

Item	Value

continued

The business plan – continued

How will you pay for these?	Value	Date
Grants		
Own resources		
Loans		
Creditors		

What credit is available from your suppliers?		
Supplier	Estimated value of monthly order	Number of days credit

What are your loan or overdraft requirements?

What are you putting in yourself?

What security will you be able to put up?

OTHER

Accountant
Address

Telephone
Solicitor
Address

Telephone

VAT registration
Insurance arrangements

The business plan – continued

Plan contents

Introduction

This could be a brief summary of your business but made as interesting as possible to gain the attention of the reader and stating what you hope to achieve in the next twelve months or more.

Business details

This must include:

○ The name and address of the business.
○ The telephone number.
○ The legal status (sole trader, partnership, limited company).

○ The type of business (beauty salon, fitness centre, diet clinic etc.).
○ The business activities and services.
○ The date the business began or is to begin if not already running.

Personal details

These would be of yourself as a sole trader or of the partners in a partnership or limited company.

○ Name, address and home telephone numbers.
○ Telephone numbers at work.
○ The qualifications held.
○ Work experience relevant to the business.
○ Previous business experience.
○ Any courses attended in relation to the setting up of the business.

o   The present or planned role in the business.

Staff details

Those you may be employing immediately.

o   Name, address.
o   Position in the business.
o   Qualifications.
o   Relevant work experience.

New staff
Any other skills needed by the business which will be required within the next year or two.

Staff costs

An estimate of the cost of employing staff and buying in new skills, to include your own salary and any partners in the business.

o   Number of staff.
o   Role in the business.
o   Cost per month.
o   Annual cost.

Services

Details of all the services on offer emphasizing anything that is different or special about the various treatments and why this business will succeed.

What percentage of the turnover will each treatment contribute, why the treatment is special and what the key selling points are.

Estimate the prices for the treatments on offer and explain how the estimates were produced. Give an approximate breakdown of the cost of providing each treatment or service.

Explain what competition there is and how your services compare with theirs.

State whether you are carrying out research into new areas which may be added to the business's list of services available in the foreseeable future.

What product lines you will be selling and how relevant they are to the treatments you are offering. State the selling price and the original cost.

The market

It is important to demonstrate that you have a positive idea of the market you are aiming your business at and you are sure that the services you are offering will sell. Therefore, the following information should be given:

o   Where is the market and does it have the potential for growth, or is it static or in decline.
o   How large is your market.
o   Identify the potential customers.
o   State the possibility of tailoring the services to meet the demands of other sectors within the market.

Make a list of:

o   Your competitors' services.
o   The prices they charge.
o   Their strengths and weaknesses.

Then state why your own are better and the advantages of your treatments and services over theirs.

State your advertising methods and how appropriate they are.

Operating the business

The information required here would encompass premises, equipment and suppliers.

Have business premises been found or are there plans to buy or lease? In the case of premises already acquired details should be given of the location, size and type of premises and whether there are any plans for future development or change.

State how much equipment will be needed and if it is to be bought or leased. Who will be supplying your goods and what the alternatives are if they fail to supply.

If the premises are leasehold, state:

o   The term of the lease.
o   What period of the lease is outstanding.
o   If there is an option to renew.
o   The present rent and when it is paid.
o   When the next rent review will be.
o   Who is responsible for all repairs.

CASHFLOW FORECAST FOR: MONTH   TO

	MONTH		MONTH		MONTH		MONTH		MONTH		MONTH		TOTALS	
RECEIPTS	BUDGET	ACTUAL	BUDGET	ACTUAL	BUDGET	ACTUAL	BUDGET	ACTUAL	BUDGET	ACTUAL	BUDGET	ACTUAL	BUDGET	ACTUAL
Cash Sales														
Cash from Debtors														
Capital Introduced														
TOTAL RECEIPTS (a)														
PAYMENTS														
Payments to Creditors														
Salaries/Wages														
Rent/Rates/Water														
Insurance														
Repairs/Renewals														
Heat/Light/Power														
Advertising														
Printing/Stationary/Postage														
Cash Purchases														
Telephone														
Professional Fees														
Capital Payments														
Interest Charges														
Other														
VAT Payable (refund)														
TOTAL PAYMENTS (b)														
NET CASHFLOW (a–b)														
OPENING BANK BALANCE														
CLOSING BANK BALANCE														

Figure 14.2 *An example of a cash flow forecast*

Future prospects

What plans you may have to cope with the growth of the business or any changes you may wish to make.

Financial details

This will provide the information required by a bank manager or investor when you wish to borrow money. There is a risk involved when lending money therefore it is important to show what assets you have available as insurance against anything going wrong along with the following information:

○   When you hope to repay the capital.
○   What funds of your own you have available.
○   Will there be any other source of funds open to you, if so who will provide them, how much will it be and when will it be available.
○   A cash flow forecast which analyses expenditure and receipts over a period of time, usually one year.

Receipts or money coming into the business would include:

○   Cash from sales.
○   Loans received.
○   Capital invested.
○   Other income (for example slimming club).

Expenditure or money paid out of the business would include:

○   Payments to suppliers.
○   Purchases.
○   Wages.
○   Insurance.
○   Rent, rates and water.
○   Services – heat, light, power, telephone.
○   Loan repayments.
○   Interest.
○   Leasing repayments.
○   Capital expenditure.
○   Advertising.
○   Professional fees.
○   Bank charges.
○   Other.

Closing bank balance is ascertained by adding the opening bank balance to the total receipts and taking away the total expenditure.

Because the cash flow forecast will be based on assumptions which form a vital part of the financial forecast, it is important to be realistic and note the assumptions made. It provides a picture to any possible investors of when you envisage money flowing in and out of your bank account over a set period of time.

From the forecast it will be evident when your need for cash is the greatest and what your funding requirements may be (Figure 14.2).

Useful terminology

Asset: Something of value owned by the business, for example property or equipment which may be sold to pay debts.
Balance sheet: A statement which shows the assets and liabilities of the business.
Capital: The amount of money in the business belonging to the owner or shareholders.
Cash book: This provides a daily record of financial transactions.
Credit: When a period of time elapses before payment is made for goods or services.
Creditor: One to whom debt is due.
Debtor: One who owes money to the business.
Depreciation: A reduction of the value of an asset over a period of time.
Facility: Bank loan or overdraft offered to a business by the bank.
Fixed costs: Overheads of the business.
Income: Money received for goods and services.
Liability: A debt within the business or a future commitment.
Liquid asset: An asset of the business which may be easily converted into cash.
Overdraft: An extension of credit given by the bank on a current account.
Statement of account: A record of all transactions over a period of time sent by a bank or a company to the business.
Stock: Goods stored for sale or use.
Trading account: A record of sales for a period plus the cost of the sales for the same period which shows the gross profit.
Working capital: The money which is used for the day-to-day running of the business.

Therapists and hairdressers today have a variety of career opportunities after they have completed a recognized course and received the necessary qualifications to put their skills into practice.

Types of work

Salons

Therapists will have the opportunity to practise facial and body treatments (manual and electrical, electrolysis and makeup) in a good beauty salon and this provides a sound base for going on to other more specialized jobs and even to consider starting their own business. The experience gained here is varied and they will learn how to sell products, keep records, supervise other members of staff, manage the salon and, most importantly, to please the client and promote the business.

Hairdressers will gain the same experience in running the salon, client care and retailing in addition to perfecting the art of cutting, styling, colouring and perming. Hairdressing is required in locations other than a high street salon and the opportunities are many and varied. Salons may be established in hotels, hospitals, airports, health farms, department stores, cruise liners, fitness and leisure clubs.

Health farms

The type of work encountered on a health farm is similar to that of a beauty salon but the hours can be much longer and there is more emphasis on body treatments and weight reduction. The therapist will also work closely with the dietician and will take exercise classes which can include yoga, aerobics, jogging or pool exercise and work in the gym providing fitness training.

Leisure centres

The work here will involve taking exercise classes and fitness training and supervising treatments such as sauna, steam and sunbeds.

Cruise liners

All treatments are now available on cruise liners but therapists are normally required to gain at least two years' experience before they are accepted. The hours are long and it is essential that the therapist is competent to work with initiative and without the need for close supervision.

Makeup artist

The areas for a makeup artist besides a salon are with a professional photographer, in a model agency or freelance. Television or film work is highly competitive and quite often the therapist will be required to serve a long apprenticeship but the work is interesting even though the hours are long. Theatres may employ makeup artists but probably on a part-time basis or in a self-employed capacity.

Theatre and television require the specialist skills of a hairdresser, in particular wigmaking and high standards in both men's and women's hairdressing. This type of work requires commitment, flexibility and initiative.

Makeup and skin care consultant

Cosmetic companies are pleased to employ beauty therapists as their background knowledge is an asset when selling makeup and skin care ranges within a store. There is also the opportunity then to work up through the ranks and become an area representative for the company, responsible for many retail outlets.

Company sales representative

Exceptional selling and communication skills are required as well as enthusiasm and stamina to be able to build up a solid client base. An area will be allocated to a sales rep with the responsibility to establish new business and maintain existing business. There will be a great deal of travelling to visit clients but if reps enjoy meeting people and they are selling products they believe in, this is a highly rewarding job. Commission is earned on all sales, therefore the harder a rep works, the higher the potential earnings.

Remedial makeup practitioner

Working in conjunction with a dermatologist or in a hospital, teaching people how to apply camouflage makeup skilfully, to conceal scars and blemishes and skin care maintenance and makeup application after plastic surgery.

Public relations

There are now many treatments offered in cosmetic surgery clinics which do not require surgery. Because of the extensive knowledge therapists have concerning the skin and beauty requirements of most women, they are an ideal person to present the services available to other therapists and to the general public. They may also help with post-operative advice to clients who may never have worn or shown an interest in makeup before because of a problem which has now been corrected.

Hair and beauty journalism

Producing articles or columns for magazines and newspapers. With a knowledge of the hair and beauty industry and the ability to write, information booklets and brochures may be produced for manufacturers.

Teaching

It is important to gain as much industrial experience as possible before embarking upon a teacher-training course. Teaching can then be full-time or part-time while still pursuing other interests within the hair and beauty field.

Franchising

Taking out a franchise to run a hairdressing salon, beauty salon or fitness club or to sell skin care products, gives hairdressers and therapists a well-known name to trade under, the training and continuing guidance of a large organization, with the advantage of independence and self-employment. The risks are not quite as great when selling a tried and tested product and the franchise operator is providing technical help and in some cases national advertising.

Technical representative

There are many companies producing beauty therapy equipment, professional skin and body care ranges as well as makeup. They employ qualified beauty therapists to demonstrate all their products to colleges and potential buyers. They also provide a follow-up service presenting new equipment and products and giving specialist training when necessary.

Mobile work

This is an ideal way of providing beauty therapy services without the overheads of business premises and many people prefer treatments in the comfort of their home. The largest capital outlay would be a car but there are limitations in the services you may offer as it would be difficult to carry a great deal of equipment. It is important to gain experience first in an established business and choose carefully the treatments you will offer. Sometimes specializing in a particular area, for example aromatherapy, is the answer as this only entails carrying a portable couch, towels and oils.

Mobile hairdressers can take their services much more easily into hospitals, residential homes or office premises especially when offering cutting and styling services instead of the more complicated colouring and perming as equipment may be carried in a reasonable sized holdall.

Specialist/consultant

There are areas of specialization which hairdressers and therapists may wish to pursue after several years of industrial experience, these may include trichology for the hairdresser specializing in treating serious hair problems or thread vein removal for the electrologist and remedial camouflage for the beauty therapist.

Index

Beauty Therapy Fact File

Second Edition

Susan Cressy

This book has been written for all ages and levels of ability and provides a comprehensive source of reference for students studying beauty therapy up to and including NVQ Levels 1, 2 and 3. This edition has been revised to include all the new course requirements for Business Management Level 3.

Beauty therapists have to acquire a great deal of knowledge when undertaking any course. This book, therefore, is an invaluable guide to principles and practices in beauty therapy since it covers all aspects of beauty therapy which are important to the trainee and practitioner.

The book is presented in a clear and concise way to enable students to find information quickly and easily. Divided into five parts, the contents include: facial treatments; body treatments; epilation and hair; manicure, pedicure and depilation; business management.

0 7506 2770 0
Paperback

Available from Heinemann Publishers Oxford on
01865 314627

Body Massage for the Beauty Therapist

Third Edition

Audrey Goldberg and Lucy McDonald

'To call the first textbook of its kind the best is an illogicality....But it must surely be a long time before we see another book on massage as instructive and easy to read as *Body Massage for the Beauty Therapist.'*
Hair and Beauty

The physical comfort and reassurance which massage can give, especially when coupled with exercises, makes it more than a sensuous luxury, rather a positive factor in promoting body well-being.

The beauty therapist, increasingly called upon to administer massage will welcome this manual. The clear and detailed explanations of massage techniques are supplemented by many drawings and new photographs integrated in the text, which also serve to make clear the structure of the human body and its functioning. The personality and qualities of the therapist are brought into perspective and helpful advice given on the organization of the salon. Valuable sections are included on relaxation techniques and correct breathing, and many new exercises, such as step, are included in the revised and expanded chapter on active exercise. The third edition also covers treatment for cellulite, hydrotherapy, vacuum suction and galvanism in the chapter on new techniques.

0 7506 2453 1
Paperback

Available from Heinemann Publishers Oxford on
01865 314627

The Principles and Practice of Electrical Epilation

Second Edition

Sheila Godfrey

Written for the practising electrolysist and student, this book covers all aspects of electro-epilation and takes into account recent changes and advances in training and technology during the past decade. These changes are wide-ranging and topics covered in the second edition include: improved standards of training; the Blend technique of electro-epilation; the development of pre-sterilized disposable needles; the advent of AIDS; the identification of hepatitis C, D and E; training and health and safety at work.

A knowledge of endocrinology, the structure and growth cycle of hair, the skin, hygiene, electricity and basic first aid is essential to an understanding of why hair growth occurs and how this problem, which causes distress to very many people, can be treated both safely and efficiently. All these topics are thoroughly covered and advice on how to set up your own practice is also given.

0 7506 2924 X
Paperback

Available from Heinemann Publishers Oxford on
01865 314627

Cutting Hair the Vidal Sassoon Way

Second Edition

The second edition of this highly successful manual has been up-dated to incorporate creations from the Vidal Sassoon International Creative Team. Through this manual their creations are now made available to hairdressers everywhere illustrating the creative talents and innovative ideas that have kept the name Vidal Sassoon in the forefront of hairdressing.

In this book the acknowledged leader in the world of hairdressing and hair care reveals the secrets and techniques that have made the Vidal Sassoon organization famous all over the world. Here you can learn exactly how the basics and most important haircuts are done step-by-step – backed by many photographs.

However, this book is no means concerned only with cutting hair. It is about the Vidal Sassoon philosophy of hair, the condition and care of hair, the way it grows and the decisive element of choosing the right style for each type of bone structure and personality. You will be able to look over the master's shoulder and study the intricacies of dealing with different kinds of hair. You will find out what equipment to use, how to blow-dry efficiently and how to make maximum use of the many practical hints from the world-wide Vidal Sassoon Creative Team. It is a book about the qualities and qualifications that make for success in the world of haircutting and hair-care. It is vital reading for every student of the craft and really required reading for every student of the craft.

07506 0324 0
Paperback

Available from Heinemann Publishers Oxford on
01865 314627